POEMS

BY

RICHARD CHENEVIX TRENCH

AUTHOR OF "THE STUDY OF WORDS"—"ENGLISH, PAST AND PRESENT"—"LESSONS ON PROVERBS"—"SYNONYMS OF THE NEW TESTAMENT"—"CALDERON," ETC

REDFIELD
34 BEEKMAN STREET, NEW YORK
1857

SAVAGE & McCREA, STEREOTYPERS,
13 Chambers Street, N. Y.

PREFACE.

In issuing the present volume, a word or two of explanation is due to the reader; and it has rarely fallen to the lot of an American Editor to have a more agreeable duty to discharge than in saying what is requisite to the occasion.

It may not be known to every one, that Richard Chenevix Trench is a poet as well as a divine; that he is one of the truest and best of the poets of our day; and that he has cultivated the muses no less successfully than the graver studies of the theologian and professor of divinity. With us, he is widely known and revered as a profound master in theological science, and a ripe and admirable scholar in polite literature. In England, he is also recognised as a poet worthy to rank with the Herberts, the Hebers, the Kebles, and others of the clergy, who have given utterance to strains of poesy as charming and soothing as they are instructive and elevating. The "Christian Remembrancer"—no mean authority—in an able article, some years ago, on "The Religious Poets of the Day," declares of Mr. Trench: "We put him at the head of our present religious poets. More than any of his brethren, he seems to us to have a distinct calling to serve the Muses. He was born a poet, and would have been one, we think, had his mind never been called to the sacred subjects which have exercised it, and which have 'moralized his strain.' He is, too, more than any of his rivals in the same line, an *artist*, nearly always seeking to *perfect* his veriest trifles. . . . . . In keeping with this great merit, we must mention the severity and purity of Mr. TRENCH's English, a praise which we can not accord to other of his contemporaries, whom, in some respects, we rate very highly."

Fully persuaded of all this, it seemed to the American Editor only meet and proper that Mr. TRENCH should be permitted to delight the lovers of poesy on this side of the Atlantic by his wooings of the muse, no less than by his noble contributions to theological and general literature. During past years he has published several volumes of poems;* and it occurred to the Editor that a copious selection from these volumes might be made, which should bring the learned and estimable author before American readers in a somewhat new but not less pleasing light. Accordingly, in the course of correspondence, he suggested the plan and its substance to Mr. TRENCH; and received in reply, not only the author's consent, but his most hearty commendation of the plan and its execution.

The selection in the present volume comprises considerably more than half of Mr. TRENCH's published poems. Confidently believing that it has been so made as not unwittingly to do injustice to the accomplished author, and not without hope that the entire collection may, at no distant day, be called for, the present volume is commended to the thousands of intelligent readers in our country who can appreciate and enjoy the rich repast here set before them.

J. A. SPENCER.

NEW YORK, *Easter Even*, 1856.

* "The Story of Justin Martyr, and other Poems." Third Edition, 1851, pp. 284.

"Poems from Eastern Sources, Genoveva, and other Poems." Second Edition, with Additions, 1851, pp. 245.

"Elegiac Poems." Second Edition, 1850, pp. 75.

"Alma, and other Poems." Second Edition, 1855, pp. 44.

CONTENTS.

THE STORY OF JUSTIN MARTYR

AND OTHER POEMS.

THE

STORY OF JUSTIN MARTYR.

SEE JUSTIN MARTYR'S FIRST DIALOGUE WITH TRYPHO.

IT seems to me like yesterday,
The morning when I took my way
Upon the shore—in solitude;
For in that miserable mood
It was relief to quit the ken
And the inquiring looks of men—
The looks of love and gentleness,
And pity, that would fain express
Its only purpose was to know,
That, knowing, it might soothe my wo:
But when I felt that I was free
From searching gaze, it was to me
Like ending of a dreary task,
Or putting off a cumbrous mask.
I wandered forth upon the shore,
Wishing this lie of life was o'er;

What was beyond I could not guess,
I thought it might be quietness,
And now I had no dream of bliss,
No thought, no other hope but this—
To be at rest;—for all that fed
The dream of my proud youth had fled,
My dream of youth that I would be
Happy and glorious, wise and free,
In mine own right, and keep my state,
And would repel the heavy weight,
The load that crushed unto the ground
The servile multitude around;
The purpose of my life had failed—
The heavenly heights I would have scaled
Seemed more than ever out of sight,
Farther beyond my feeble flight.
The beauty of the universe
Was lying on me like a curse;
Only the lone surge at my feet
Uttered a soothing murmur sweet,
As every broken weary wave
Sunk gently to a quiet grave,
Dying on the bosom of the sea:
And death grew beautiful to me,
Until it seemed a mother mild,
And I like some too happy child—
A happy child, that, tired with play,
Through a long summer holyday,

Runs to his mother's arms to weep
His little weariness asleep.
Rest—rest—all passion that once stirred
My heart, had ended in one word—
My one desire to be at rest,
To lay my head on any breast,
Where there was hope that I might keep
A dreamless and unbroken sleep;
And the lulled Ocean seemed to say,
"With me is quiet—come away."
There was a tale which oft had stirred
My bosom deeply: you have heard
How that the treacherous sea-maid's art
With song inveigles the lost heart
Of some lone fisher, that has stood
For days beside the glimmering flood;
And when has grown upon him there
The mystery of earth and air,
He can not find with whom to part
The burden lying at his heart;
So when the mermaid bids him come,
And summons to her peaceful home,
He hears—he leaps into the wave,
To find a home, and not a grave.
It stirred me now—and sweet seemed death;
The ceasing of this painful breath,
The laying down this life of care,
The breathing of a purer air—

Sweet seemed they all—a richer thing
Death, than whatever life could bring.

Anon I said I would not die;
I loathed to live—I feared to die—
So I went forward, till I stood
Amid a marble solitude,
A ruined town of ancient day.
I rested where some steps away
From other work of human hand
Two solitary pillars stand—
Two pillars on a mild hillside,
Like sea-marks of a shrunken tide:
Their shafts were by the sea-breeze worn,
Beneath them waved the verdant corn!
But a few paces from the crown
Of that green summit, farther down,
A fallen pillar on the plain,
Slow sinking in the earth again,
Bedding itself in dark, black mould,
Lay moveless where it first had rolled.
It once had been a pillar high,
And pointing to the starry sky;
But now lay prostrate, its own weight
Now serving but to fix its state,
To sink it in its earthly bed.
I gazed, and to myself I said:—
"This pillar lying on the plain
The hand of man might raise again,

And set it as in former days;
But the fall'n spirit who shall raise—
What power on earth? what power in heaven?"
How quickly was an answer given
Unto this voice of my despair!
But now I sat in silence there,
I thought upon the vanished time,
And my irrevocable prime,
My baffled purpose, wasted years,
My sin, my misery—and my tears
Fell thick and fast upon the sands;
I hid my face within my hands,
For tears are strange that find their way
Under the open eye of day,
Under the broad and glorious sun,
Full in the heavens, as mine have done,
And as upon that day they did,
Unnoticed, unrestrained, unchid.
How long I might have felt them flow
Without a check, I do not know;
But presently, while yet I kept
That attitude of wo, and wept,
A mild voice sounded in mine ears—
"You can not wash your heart with tears!"
I quickly turned—and vexed to be
Seen in my spirit's agony,
In anger had almost replied—
An aged man was at my side.

I think that since my life began,
I never saw an older man
Than he who stood beside me then,
And with mild accents said again:—
"You can not cleanse your heart with tears,
Though you should weep as many years
As our great Father, when he sat
Uncomforted on Ararat—
This would not help you, and the tear
Which does not heal, will scald and sear.
What is your sorrow?"

Until now
I never had unveiled my wo—
Not that I shunned sweet sympathies,
Man's words, or woman's pitying eyes;
But that I felt they were in vain,
And could not help me; for the pain
The wound which I was doomed to feel,
Man gave not, and he could not heal.
But in this old man's speech and tone
Was something that allured me on;
I told him all—I did not hide
My sin, my sorrow, or my pride:
I told him how, when I began
First to verge upward to a man,
These thoughts were mine—to dwell alone,
My spirit on its lordly throne,

Hating the vain stir, fierce and loud,
The din of the tumultuous crowd;
And how I thought to arm my soul,
And 'stablish it in self-control;
And said I would obey the right,
And would be strong in wisdom's might,
And bow unto my own heart's law,
And keep my heart from speck or flaw,
That in its mirror I might find
A reflex of the Eternal mind,
A glass to give me back the truth;
And how before me from my youth
A phantom ever on the wing,
Appearing now, now vanishing,
Had flitted, looking out from shrine,
From painting, or from work divine
Of poet's or of sculptor's art;
And how I feared it might depart,
That beauty which alone could shed
Light on my life—and then I said,
I would beneath its shadow dwell,
And would all lovely things compel,
All that was beautiful or fair
In art or nature, earth or air,
To be as ministers to me,
To keep me pure, to keep me free
From worldly service, from the chain
Of custom, and from earthly stain;

And how they kept me for a while,
And did my foolish heart beguile;
Yet all at last did faithless prove,
And, late or soon, betrayed my love;
How they had failed me one by one,
Till now, my youth yet scarcely done,
The heart, which I had thought to steep
In hues of beauty, and to keep
Its consecrated home and fane,
That heart was soiled with many a stain,
Which from without and from within
Had gathered there till all was sin,
Till now I only drew my breath—
I lived but in the hope of death.

While my last words were giving place
To my heart's anguish, o'er his face
A shadow of displeasure past
But vanished then again as fast
As the breeze-shadow from the brook;
And with mild words and pitying look
He gently said:—
"Ah me, my son,
A weary course your life has run;
And yet it need not be in vain
That you have suffered all this pain;
And if my years might make me bold
To speak, methinks I could unfold

Why in such efforts you could meet
But only misery and defeat.
Yet deem not of us as at strife,
Because you set before your life
A purpose and a loftier aim,
Than the blind lives of men may claim
For the most part—or that you sought,
By fixed resolve and solemn thought,
To lift your being's calm estate
Out of the range of time and fate.
Glad am I that a thing unseen,
A spiritual Presence, this has been
Your worship, this your young heart stirred.
But yet herein you proudly erred,
Here may the source of wo be found:
You thought to fling, yourself around,
The atmosphere of light and love
In which it was your joy to move;
You thought by efforts of your own
To take at last each jarring tone
Out of your life, till all should meet
In one majestic music sweet;
And deemed that in our own heart's ground
The root of good was to be found,
And that by careful watering
And earnest tendance we might bring
The bud, the blossom, and the fruit,
To grow and flourish from that root—

You deemed we needed nothing more
Than skill and courage to explore
Deep down enough in our own heart,
To where the well-head lay apart,
Which must the springs of being feed,
And that these fountains did but need
The soil that choked them moved away,
To bubble in the open day.
But, thanks to Heaven, it is not so!—
That root a richer soil doth know
Than our poor hearts could e'er supply;
That stream is from a source more high:
From God it came, to God returns,
Not nourished from our scanty urns,
But fed from his unfailing river,
Which runs and will run on for ever."

When now he came to heavenly things,
And spake of them, his spirit had wings,
His words seemed not his own, but given—
I could have deemed one spake from heaven
Of hope and joy, of life and death,
And immortality through faith;
Of that great change commenced within,
The blood that cleanses from all sin,
That can wash out the inward stain,
And consecrate the heart again;
The voice that clearer and more clear
Doth speak unto the purgèd ear,

The gracious influences given
In a continued stream from heaven;
The balm that can the soul's hurt heal,
The Spirit's witness and its seal.

I listened, for unto mine ear
The word which I had longed to hear,
Was come at last, the lifeful word
Which I had often almost heard
In some deep silence of my breast—
For with a sense of dim unrest
That word unborn had often wrought,
And struggled in the womb of thought,
As from beneath the smothering earth
The seed strives upward to a birth:
And lo! it now was born indeed—
Here was the answer to my need.

But now we parted, never more
To meet upon that lone seashore.
We have not met on earth again,
And scarcely shall; there doth remain
A time, a place where we shall meet,
And have the stars beneath our feet.
Since then I many times have sought
Who this might be, and sometimes thought
It must have been an angel sent
To be a special instrument

And minister of grace to me;
Or deemed again it might be he,
Of whom some say he shall not die,
Till he have seen with mortal eye
The glory of his Lord again:
But this is a weak thought and vain.

We parted, each upon our way—
I homeward, where my glad course lay
Beside those ruins where I sate
On the same morning—desolate,—
With scarcely strength enough to grieve:
And now it was a marvellous eve,
The waters at my feet were bright,
And breaking into isles of light;
The misty sunset did enfold
A thousand floating motes of gold;
The red light seemed to penetrate
Through the worn stone, and re-create
The old, to glorify anew;
And, steeping all things through and through,
A rich dissolving splendor poured
Through rent and fissure, and restored
The fall'n, the falling, and decayed,
Filling the rifts which Time had made,
Till the rent masses seemed to meet,
The pillar stand upon its feet,
And tower and cornice, roof and stair,
Hung self-upheld in the magic air.

Transfigured thus those temples stood
Upon the margin of the flood,
All glorious as they rose of yore,
There standing, as not ever more
They could be harmed by touch of time,
But still, as in that perfect prime,
Must flourish unremoved and free,
Or, as they then appeared to me,
A newer and more glorious birth,
A city of that other earth,
That Earth which is to be.

THE MONK AND BIRD.

I.

AS he who finds one flower sharp thorns among,
  Plucks it, and highly prizes, though before
Careless regard on thousands he has flung,
  As fair as this or more:

II.

Not otherwise perhaps this argument
  Won from me, where I found it, such regard,
That I esteemed no labor thereon spent
  As wearisome or hard.

III.

In huge and antique volume did it lie,
  That by two solemn clasps was duly bound,
As neither to be opened nor laid by
  But with due thought profound.

IV.

There fixèd thought to questions did I lend,
  Which hover on the bounds of mortal ken,
And have perplexed, and will unto the end
  Perplex the brains of men:

V.

Of what is time, and what eternity,
Of all that seems and is not—forms of things—
Till my tired spirit followed painfully
On flagging, weary wings:

VI.

So that I welcomed this one resting-place,
Pleased as a bird, that, when its forces fail,
Lights panting in the ocean's middle space,
Upon a sunny sail.

VII.

And now the grace of fiction, which has power
To render things impossible believed,
And win them with the credence of an hour
To be for truths received—

VIII.

That grace must help me, as it only can,
Winning such transient credence, while I tell
What to a cloistered, solitary man
In distant times befell.

IX.

Him little might our earthly grandeur feed,
Who to the uttermost was vowed to be
A follower of his Master's barest need
In holy poverty.

X.

Nor might he know the gentle mutual strife
  Of home-affections, which can more or less
Temper with sweet the bitter of our life,
  And lighten its distress.

XI.

Yet we should err to deem that he was left
  To bear alone our being's lonely weight,
Or that his soul was vacant and bereft
  Of pomp and inward state:

XII.

Morn, when before the sun his orb unshrouds,
  Swift as a beacon-torch the light has sped,
Kindling the dusky summits of the clouds
  Each to a fiery red—

XIII.

The slanted columns of the noonday light,
  Let down into the bosom of the hills,
Or, sunset, that with golden vapor bright
  The purple mountains fills—

XIV.

These made him say—"If God has so arrayed
  A fading world that quickly passes by,
Such rich provision of delight has made
  For every human eye—

XV.

“What shall the eyes that wait for him survey,
  Where his own presence gloriously appears
In worlds that were not founded for a day,
  But for eternal years?”

XVI.

And if at seasons this world’s undelight
  Oppressed him, or the hollow at its heart,
One glance at those enduring mansions bright
  Made gloomier thoughts depart:

XVII.

Till many times the sweetness of the thought
  Of an eternal country—where it lies
Removed from care and mortal anguish, brought
  Sweet tears into his eyes.

XVIII.

Thus, not unsolaced, he longwhile abode,
  Filling all dreary, melancholy time,
And empty spaces of the heart, with God,
  And with this hope sublime:

XIX.

Even thus he lived, with little joy or pain
  Drawn through the channels by which men receive—
Most men receive the things which for the main
  Make them rejoice or grieve.

XX.

But for delight, on spiritual gladness fed,
  And obvious to temptations of like kind;
One such, from out his very gladness bred,
  It was his lot to find.

XXI.

When first it came, he lightly put it by,
  But it returned again to him ere long,
And ever hanging got some new ally,
  And every time more strong—

XXII.

A little worm that gnawed the life away
  Of a tall plant, the canker of its root,
Or like as when, from some small speck, decay
  Spreads o'er a beauteous fruit.

XXIII.

For still the doubt came back—"Can God provide
  For the large heart of man what shall not pall,
Nor through eternal ages' endless tide
  On tired spirits fall?

XXIV.

"Here but one look tow'rd heaven will oft repress
  The crushing weight of undelightful care;
But what were there beyond, if weariness
  Should ever enter there?

XXV.

" Yet do not sweetest things here soonest cloy?
Satiety the life of joy would kill,
If sweet with bitter, pleasure with annoy,
Were not attempered still."

XXVI.

This mood endured, till every act of love,
Vigils of praise and prayer, and midnight choir,
All shadows of the service done above,
And which, while his desire—

XXVII.

And while his hope was heavenward, he had loved,
As helps to disengage him from the chain
That fastens unto earth—all these now proved
Most burdensome and vain.

XXVIII.

What must have been the issue of that mood
It were a thing to fear—but that one day,
Upon the limits of an ancient wood,
His thoughts him led astray.

XXIX.

Darkling he went, nor once applied his ear,
(On a loud sea of agitations thrown),
Nature's low tones and harmonies to hear,
Heard by the calm alone.

XXX.

The merry chirrup of the grasshopper,
Sporting among the roots of withered grass,
The dry leaf rustling to the wind's light stir,
Did each unnoted pass:

XXXI.

He, walking in a trance of selfish care,
Not once observed the beauty shed around,
The blue above, the music in the air,
The flowers upon the ground:

XXXII.

Till from the centre of that forest dim
Came to him such sweet singing of a bird,
As, sweet in very truth, then seemed to him
The sweetest ever heard.

XXXIII.

That lodestar drew him onward, inward still,
Deeper than where the village-children stray.
Deeper than where the woodman's glittering bill
Lops the large boughs away—

XXXIV.

Into a central space of glimmering shade,
Where hardly might the struggling sunbeams pass,
Which a faint lattice-work of light had made
Upon the long, lank grass.

XXXV.

He did not sit, but stood and listened there,
And to him listening the time seemed not long,
While that sweet bird above him filled the air
With its melodious song.

XXXVI.

He heard not, saw not, felt not aught beside,
Through the wide worlds of pleasure and of pain,
Save the full flowing and the ample tide
Of that celestial strain.

XXXVII.

As though a bird of Paradise should light
A moment on a twig of this bleak earth,
And, singing songs of Paradise, invite
All hearts to holy mirth—

XXXVIII.

And then take wing to Paradise again,
Leaving all listening spirits raised above
The toil of earth, the trouble, and the pain,
And melted all in love:

XXXIX.

Such hidden might, such power was in the sound;
But when it ceased sweet music to unlock,
The spell that held him sense and spirit bound
Dissolved with a slight shock.

XL.

All things around were as they were before—
The trees, and the blue sky, and sunshine bright,
Painting the pale and leafstrewn forest-floor
With patches of faint light.

XLI.

But as when music doth no longer thrill,
Light shudderings yet along the chords will run,
Or the heart vibrates tremulously still,
After its prayer be done—

XLII.

So his heart fluttered all the way he went,
Listening each moment for the vesper-bell;
For a long hour he deemed he must have spent
In that untrodden dell.

XLIII.

And once it seemed that something new or strange
Had passed upon the flowers, the trees, the ground;
Some slight but unintelligible change
On everything around:

XLIV.

Such change, where all things undisturbed remain,
As only to the eye of him appears,
Who, absent long, at length returns again—
The silent work of years.

XLV.

And ever grew upon him more and more
  Fresh marvel—for, unrecognised of all,
He stood a stranger at the convent-door:
  New faces filled the hall!

XLVI.

Yet was it long ere he received the whole
  Of that strange wonder—how, while he had stood
Lost in deep gladness of his inmost soul,
  Far hidden in that wood—

XLVII.

Three generations had gone down unseen
  Under the thin partition that is spread—
The thin partition of thin earth—between
  The living and the dead!

XLVIII.

Nor did he many days to earth belong;
  For, like a pent-up stream, released again,
The years arrested by the strength of song
  Came down on him amain—

XLIX.

Sudden as a dissolving thaw in spring;
  Gentle as when upon the first warm day,
Which sunny April in its train may bring,
  The snow melts all away.

L.

They placed him in his former cell, and there
  Watched him departing; what few words he said
Were of calm peace and gladness, with one care
  Mingled—one only dread—

LI.

Lest an eternity should not suffice
  To take the measure and the breadth and height
Of what there is reserved in Paradise—
  Its ever-new delight.

TO A CHILD PLAYING.

DEAR boy, thy momentary laughter rings
  Sincerely out, and that spontaneous glee,
Seeming to need no hint from outward things,
  Breaks forth in sudden shoutings, loud and free.

From what hid fountains doth thy joyance flow,
  That borrows nothing from the world around?
Its springs must deeper lie than we can know,
  A well whose springs lie safely underground.

So be it ever—and, thou happy boy,
  When time, that takes these wild delights away,
Gives thee a measure of sedater joy,
  Which, unlike this, shall ever with thee stay:

Then may that joy, like this, to outward things
  Owe nothing, but lie safe beneath the sod,
A hidden fountain fed from unseen springs,
  From the glad-making river of our God.

A WALK IN A CHURCHYARD.

WE walked within the churchyard bounds,
My little boy and I—
He laughing, running happy rounds,
I pacing mournfully.

"Nay, child! it is not well," I said,
"Among the graves to shout,
To laugh and play among the dead,
And make this noisy rout."

A moment to my side he clung,
Leaving his merry play,
A moment stilled his joyous tongue,
Almost as hushed as they:

Then, quite forgetting the command
In life's exulting burst
Of early glee, let go my hand,
Joyous as at the first.

And now I did not check him more,
  For, taught by Nature's face,
I had grown wiser than before
  Even in that moment's space:

She spread no funeral-pall above
  That patch of churchyard ground,
But the same azure vault of love
  As hung o'er all around.

And white clouds o'er that spot would pass,
  As freely as elsewhere;
The sunshine on no other grass
  A richer hue might wear.

And formed from out that very mould
  In which the dead did lie,
The daisy with its eye of gold
  Looked up into the sky.

The rook was wheeling overhead,
  Nor hastened to be gone—
The small bird did its glad notes shed,
  Perched on a gray head-stone.

And God, I said, would never give
  This light upon the earth,
Nor bid in childhood's heart to live
  These springs of gushing mirth—

If our one wisdom were to mourn,
  And linger with the dead,
To nurse, as wisest, thoughts forlorn
  Of worm and earthy bed.

Oh, no! the glory earth puts on,
  The child's unchecked delight,
Both witness to a triumph won,
  (If we but read aright) —

A triumph won o'er sin and death,
  From these the Savior saves;
And, like a happy infant, Faith
  Can play among the graves.

TO ——,

ON THE MORNING OF HER BAPTISM.

THIS will we name thy better birthday, child,
O born already to a sin-worn world,
But now unto a kingdom undefiled,
Where over thee Love's banner is unfurled.

Lo! on the morning of this holy day
I lay aside the weight of human fears,
Which I had for thee, and without dismay
Look through the avenue of coming years:

I see thee passing without mortal harm
Through ranks of foes against thy safety met;
I see thee passing — thy defence and charm,
The seal of God upon thy forehead set.

From this time forth thou often shalt hear say
Of what immortal City thou wert given
The rights and full immunities to-day,
And of the hope laid up for thee in heaven:

From this time forward thou shalt not believe
That thou art earthly, or that aught of earth,
Or aught that hell can threaten, shall receive
Power on the children of the second birth.

O risen out of death into the day
Of an immortal life, we bid thee hail,
And will not kiss the water-drops away,
The dew that rests upon thy forehead pale.

And if the seed of better life lie long,
As in a wintry hiddenness and death,
Then calling back this day, we will be strong
To wait in hope for Heaven's reviving breath:

To water, if there should be such sad need,
The undiscernèd germ with sorrowing tears;
To wait until from that undying seed
Out of the earth a heavenly plant appears:

The growth and produce of a fairer land,
And thence transplanted to a barren soil,
It needs the tendance of a careful hand—
Of Love, that is not weary with long toil:

And thou, dear child, whose very helplessness
Is as a bond upon us and a claim,
Mayest thou have this of us, as we no less
Have daily from our Father known the same.

TO MY GODCHILD.

ON THE DAY OF HIS BAPTISM.

NO harsh transitions Nature knows,
No dreary spaces intervene;
Her work in silence forward goes,
And rather felt than seen:

For where the watcher, that with eye
Turned eastward, yet could ever say
When the faint glooming in the sky
First lightened into day?

Or maiden, by an opening flower
That many a summer morn has stood,
Could fix upon the very hour
It ceased to be a bud?

The rainbow-colors mix and blend
Each with the other, until none
Can tell where fainter hues had end,
And deeper tints begun.

But only doth this much appear—
  That the pale hues are deeper grown;
The day has broken bright and clear;
  The bud is fully blown.

Dear child, and happy shalt thou be,
  If from this hour with just increase
All good things shall grow up in thee,
  By such unmarked degrees:

If there shall be no dreary space
  Between thy present self and past,
No dreary, miserable place
  With spectral shapes aghast:

But the full graces of thy prime
  Shall, in their weak beginnings, be
Lost in an unremembered time
  Of holy infancy.

This blessing is the first and best;
  Yet has not prayer been made in vain
For them, though not so amply blest,
  The lost and found again.

And shouldest thou, alas! forbear
  To choose the better, nobler lot,
Yet may we not esteem our prayer
  Unheard or heeded not:

If after many a wandering,
  And many a devious pathway trod,
If having known that bitter thing,
  To leave the Lord thy God—

It yet shall be, that thou at last,
  Although thy noon be lost, return
To bind life's eve in union fast
  With this, its blessèd morn.

TO AN INFANT SLEEPING.

I.

OH, drinking deep of slumber's holy wine,
  Whence may the smile that lights thy countenance be?
We seek in vain the mystery to divine,
  For in thy dim, unconscious infancy
No games as yet, no playfellows are thine,
  To stir in waking hours such thoughts of glee,
As, recollected in thine innocent dream,
Might shed across thy face this happy gleam.

II.

It may be, though small notice thou canst take,
  Thou feelest that an atmosphere of love
Is ever round thee, sleeping or awake:
  Thou wakest, and kind faces from above
Bend o'er thee; when thou sleepest, for thy sake
  All sounds are hushed, and each doth gently move:
And this dim consciousness of tender care
Has caused thy cheek this light of joy to wear.

III.

Or it may be, thoughts deeper than we deem
  Visit an infant's slumbers: God is near,
Angels are talking to them in their dream,
  Angelic voices whispering sweet and clear:
And round them lies that region's holy gleam,
  But newly left, and light which is not here;
And thus has come that smile upon thy face,
At tidings brought thee from thy native place.

IV.

But whatsoe'er the causes which beguiled
  That dimple on thy countenance, it is gone;
Fair is the lake disturbed by ripple mild,
  But not less fair when ripple it has none:
And now what deep repose is thine, dear child,
  What smoothness thy unruffled cheek has won!
Oh! who that gazed upon thee could forbear
The silent breathing of a heart-felt prayer!

TO E———.

MUCH have we to support us in our strife
With things which else would crush us, nor alone
Secret refreshings of the inward life,
But many a flower of sweetest scent is strown
Upon our outward and our open way;
None sweeter than are at some seasons known
To them who dwell for many a prosperous day
Under one roof, and have, as they would hope,
One purpose for their lives, one aim, one scope—
To labor upward on the path to heaven.
Full of refreshment these occasions are,
Like seasonable resting-places given
To pilgrim feet; for though, alas! too rare,
Yet the sweet memories they supply, will give
The food on which affection's heart may live
In after-times; since it were sad indeed
If all more intimate knowledge did not breed
More trust in one another and more love,
More faith that each is seeking to attain
With humble, earnest effort, not in vain,

The happy rest of God. And so they part
On their divided ways with cheerful heart,
Knowing that in all places they will call
On the same God and Father over all;
And part not wholly, since they meet whose prayer
Meets at the throne of Heaven; one life divine
Through all the branches of the mystical vine
Flows ever, even as the same breath of air
Lifts every leaflet of a mighty grove.
And from our meeting we shall reap a share
Of a yet higher good, if we have won
Hereby the strengthening of one weak desire,
The fanning of one faint spark to a fire,
The stirring of one prayer that we may prove
Steadfast and faithful till our work be done,
Until the course appointed us be run.

We know not whither our frail barks are borne,
To quiet haven, or on stormy shore;
Nor need we seek to know it, while above
The tempest and the waters' angriest roar
Are heard the voices of almighty love—
So we shall find none dreary nor forlorn.
Whither we go we know not, but we know
That if we keep our faces surely set
Towàrd new Zion, we shall reach at last,
When every danger, every wo is past,
The city where the sealèd tribes are met,

Whither the nations of the savèd flow—
The city with its heaven-descended halls,
The city builded round with diamond walls.

Then how should we feel sorrow or dim fear
At any parting now, if there to meet?
How should our hearts with sadder pulses beat,
When thou art going where kind hearts will greet
And welcome thy return, and there as here
Thou still wilt find thine own appointed sphere,
To fill the measure up of gentle deeds—
Even as we have learnèd that in these,
That in the holy Christian charities,
And the suppliance of the lowliest needs
Of the most lowly, our true greatness is!

Therefore we will not seek to win thy stay,
Nor ask but this—that thou shouldst bear away
Kind memories of us, and only claim
What of thyself thou wilt be prompt to give,
That in thy heart's affections he may live,
To whom thou bearest that most holy name
Of spiritual mother. O beloved friend,
It is a cheering thought, if I should be
Where I can no more watch for him nor tend
His infant years—there where I can not see
What good, what evil wait upon his way—
That yet thy love, thy counsel, and thy cares,
He will not lack, a child of faithful prayers.

TO A FRIEND,

ENTERING THE MINISTRY.

I.

HIGH thoughts at first, and visions high
  Are ours of easy victory;
The word we bear seems so divine,
So framed for Adam's guilty line,
  That none, unto ourselves we say,
Of all his sinning, suffering race,
Will hear that word, so full of grace,
  And coldly turn away.

II.

But soon a sadder mood comes round—
High hopes have fallen to the ground,
And the embassadors of peace
Go weeping, that men will not cease
  To strive with Heaven—they inly mourn,
That suffering men will not be blest,
That weary men refuse to rest,
  And wanderers to return.

III.

Well is it, if has not ensued
Another, yet unworthier, mood,
When all unfaithful thoughts have way,
When we hang down our hands, and say—
"Alas! it is a weary pain
To seek with toil and fruitless strife,
To chafe the numbed limbs into life,
That will not live again."

IV.

Then if Spring-odors on the wind
Float by, they bring into our mind
That it were wiser done, to give
Our hearts to Nature, and to live
For her—or in the student's bower
To search into her hidden things,
And seek in books the wondrous springs
Of knowledge and of power.

V.

Or if we dare not thus draw back,
Yet oh! to shun the crowded track
And the rude throng of men!—to dwell
In hermitage or lonely cell,
Feeding all longings that aspire
Like incense heavenward, and with care
And lonely vigil nursing there
Faith's solitary pyre.

VI.

Oh! let not us this thought allow—
The heat, the dust upon our brow,
Signs of the contest, we may wear:
Yet thus we shall appear more fair
  In our Almighty Master's eye,
Than if in fear to lose the bloom,
Or ruffle the soul's lightest plume,
  We from the strife should fly.

VII.

And for the rest, in weariness,
In disappointment, or distress,
When strength decays, or hope grows dim,
We ever may recur to Him,
  Who has the golden oil divine,
Wherewith to feed our failing urns—
Who watches every lamp that burns
  Before his sacred shrine.

"REJOICE EVERMORE."

I.

BUT how shall we be glad?
We that are journeying through a vale of tears,
Encompassed with a thousand woes and fears,
How should we not be sad?

II.

Angels, that ever stand
Within the presence-chamber, and there raise
The never-interrupted hymn of praise,
May welcome this command:

III.

Or they whose strife is o'er,
Who all their weary length of life have trod,
As pillars now within the temple of God,
That shall go out no more.

IV.

But we who wander here,
We that are exiled in this gloomy place,
Still doomed to water Earth's unthankful face
With many a bitter tear—

V.

Bid us lament and mourn,
Bid us that we go mourning all the day,
And we will find it easy to obey,
Of our best things forlorn:

VI.

But not that we be glad;
If it be true the mourners are the blest,
Oh, leave us in a world of sin, unrest,
And trouble, to be sad!

VII.

I spake, and thought to weep—
For sin and sorrow, suffering and crime,
That fill the world, all mine appointed time
A settled grief to keep.

VIII.

When lo! as day from night,
As day from out the womb of night forlorn,
So from that sorrow was that gladness born,
Even in mine own despite.

IX.

Yet was not that by this
Excluded—at the coming of that joy
Fled not that grief—nor did that grief destroy
The newly-risen bliss:

X.

But side by side they flow,
Two fountains flowing from one smitten heart,
And ofttimes scarcely to be known apart—
That gladness and that wo:

XI.

Two fountains from one source,
Or which from two such neighboring sources run,
That aye for him who shall unseal the one,
The other flows perforce.

XII.

And both are sweet and calm,
Fair flowers upon the banks of either blow,
Both fertilize the soil, and where they flow
Shed round them holy balm.

SONNET.

OUR course is onward, onward into light:
What though the darkness gathereth amain,
Yet to return or tarry both are vain.
How tarry, when around us is thick night?
Whither return? what flower yet ever might,
In days of gloom, and cold, and stormy rain,
Enclose itself in its green bud again,
Hiding from wrath of tempest out of sight?
Courage!—we travel through a darksome cave;
But still, as nearer to the light we draw,
Fresh gales will reach us from the upper air,
And wholesome dews of heaven our foreheads lave,
The darkness lighten more, till full of awe
We stand in the open sunshine—unaware.

SONNET.

WHAT is the greatness of a fallen king?
This—that his fall avails not to abate
His spirit to a level with his fate,
Or inward fall along with it to bring;
That he disdains to stoop his former wing,
But keeps in exile and in want the law
Of kingship yet, and counts it scorn to draw
Comfort indign from any meaner thing.
Soul, that art fallen from thine ancient place,
Mayest thou in this mean world find nothing great,
Nor aught that shall the memories efface
Of that true greatness which was once thine own,
As knowing thou must keep thy kingly state,
If thou wouldst reascend thy kingly throne.

THE HERRING-FISHERS OF LOCHFYNE.

DEEM not these fishers idle, though by day
You hear the snatches of their lazy song,
And see them listlessly the sunlight long
Strew the curved beach of this indented bay:
So deemed I, till I viewed their trim array
Of boats last night—a busy armament,
With sails as dark as ever Theseus bent
Upon his fatal rigging, take their way.
Rising betimes, I could not choose but look
For their return; and when along the lake
The morning mists were curling, saw them make
Homeward, returning toward their quiet nook,
With draggled nets down-hanging to the tide,
Weary, and leaning o'er their vessels' side.

3*

IN THE ISLE OF MULL.

THE clouds are gathering in their western dome,
Deep-drenched with sunlight, as a fleece with dew,
While I with baffled effort still pursue
And track these waters toward their mountain-home,
In vain — though cataract, and mimic foam,
And island-spots, round which the streamlet threw
Its sister-arms, which joyed to meet anew,
Have lured me on, and won me still to roam;
Till now, coy nymph, unseen thy waters pass,
Or faintly struggle through the twinkling grass —
And I, thy founts unvisited, return.
Is it that thou art revelling with thy peers?
Or dost thou feed a solitary urn,
Else unreplenished, with thine own sad tears?

THE SAME.

SWEET Water-nymph, more shy than Arethuse,
 Why wilt thou hide from me thy green retreat,
Where duly thou with silver-sandalled feet,
And every Naiad, her green locks profuse,
Welcome with dance sad Evening, or unloose,
To share your revel, an oak-cinctured throng,
Oread and Dryad, who the daylight long
By rock, or cave, or antique forest, use
To shun the Wood-god and his rabble bold?
Such comes not now, or who with impious strife
Would seek to untenant meadow, stream, and plain,
Of that indwelling power which is the life
And which sustaineth each, which poets old
As god and goddess thus have loved to feign.

AN EVENING IN FRANCE.

ONE star is shining in the crimson eve,
And the thin texture of the faint blue sky
Above is like a veil intensely drawn;
Upon the spirit with a solemn weight
The marvel and the mystery of eve
Is lying, as all holy thoughts and calm,
By the vain stir and tumult of the day
Chased far away, come back on tranquil wing,
Like doves returning to their noted haunts.
It is the solemn even-tide—the hour
Of holy musings, and to us no less
Of sweet refreshment for the bodily frame
Than for the spirit, harassed both and worn
With a long day of travel; and methinks
It must have been an evening such as this,
After a day of toilsome journeyings o'er,
When looking out on Tiber, as we now
Look out on this fair river flowing by,
Together sat the saintly Monica,*

* See Augustine's Confessions, B. 9, C. 10.

And with her, given unto her prayers, that son,
The turbid stream of whose tumultuous youth
Now first was running clear, and bright, and smooth;
And solitary sitting in the niche
Of a deep window, held delightful talk—
Such as they never could have known before,
While a deep chasm, deeper than natural love
Could e'er bridge over, lay betwixt their souls—
Of what must be the glorious life in heaven.
And looking forth on meadow, stream, and sky,
And on the golden west, that richest glow
Of sunset to the uncreated light,
Which must invest for ever those bright worlds,
Seemed darkness, and the best that earth can give,
Its noblest pleasures, they with one consent
Counted as vile, nor once to be compared—
Oh! rather say not worthy to be named
With what is to be looked for there; and thus
Leaving behind them all things which are seen,
By many a stately stair they did ascend
Above the earth and all created things,
The sun and starry heavens—yea, and above
The mind of man, until they did attain
Where light no shadow has, and life no death,
Where past or future are not, nor can be,
But an eternal present, and the Lamb
His people feeds from indeficient streams.
Then pausing for a moment, to drink in

That river of delights, at length they cried:—
"Oh! to be thus for ever, and to hear
Thus in the silence of the lower world,
And in the silence of all thoughts that keep
Vain stir within, unutterable words,
And with the splendor of his majesty,
Whose seat is in the middle of the throne,
Thus to be fed for ever—this must be
The beatific vision, the third heaven!
What we have for these passing moments known,
To know the same for ever—this would be
That life whereof even now we held debate:
When will it be? oh! when?"

These things they said,
And for a season breathed immortal air,
But then perforce returned to earth again,
To this inferior region, while the air
Upon those highest summits is too fine
For our long breathing, while we yet have on
Our gross investiture of mortal weeds.
Yet not for nothing had their spirits flown
To those high regions, bringing back at once
A reconcilement with the mean things here,
And a more earnest longing for what there
Of nobler was by partial glimpses thus
Seen through the crannies of the prison-house.
And she, that mother—such entire content

Possessed her bosom, and her Lord had filled
The orb of her desires so round and full,
Had answered all her prayers for her lost son
With such an overmeasure of his grace,
She had no more to ask, and did not know
Why she should tarry any longer here,
Nor what she did on earth. Thus then she felt,
And to these thoughts which overflowed her heart
Gave thankful utterance meet; nor many days
After this vision and foretaste of joy,
Inherited the substance of the things
Which she had seen, and entered into peace.

THE DESCENT OF THE RHONE.

OFTEN when my thought has been
Pondering on what sight once seen,
Which of all the glorious shows
Nature can at will disclose,
Once beholden would supply
To the spirit's inward eye,
Most unfailing treasures, which
Would the memory most enrich
With its spectacles of power—
It has seemed no ampler dower
Of her sights and solemn shows
She to any to disclose
Than to them, who night and day—
An illimitable way—
Should sail down some mighty river,
Sailing as to sail for ever.

Lo! my wish is almost won:
Broadly flows the stately Rhone,
And we loosen from the shore
Our light pinnace, long before

The young East in gorgeous state
Has unlocked his ruby gate,
And our voyage is not done
At the sinking of the sun;
But for us the azure Night
Feeds her golden flocks with light:
All the changeful hues of heaven,
Sights and sounds of morn and even—
All unto our eyes are given.
In our view the day is born;
First the stars of lustre shorn,
Until Hesper, he who last
Kept his splendor, now fades fast;
O'er the heaven faint bloom is spread,
And the clouds blush deeper red,
Till from them the stream below
Catches the same roseate glow;
Lightens the pale east to gold,
And the west is with the fold
Of the mantle of dim Night
Scarcely darkened or less bright—
Till, his way prepared, at length,
Rising up in golden strength,
Tramples the victorious sun
The dying stars out, one by one.

Fairer scene the opening eye
Of the day can scarce descry,

Fairer sight he looks not on
Than the pleasant banks of Rhone;
Where in terraces and ranks,
On those undulating banks,
Rise by many a hilly stair
Sloping tiers of vines, where'er
From the steep and stony soil
Has been won by careful toil,
And with long, laborious pains
Fenced against the washing rains—
Fenced and anxiously walled round,
Some small patch of garden-ground.
Higher still some place of power,
Or a solitary tower,
Ruined now, is looking down
On the quiet little town
In a sheltered glen beneath,
Where the smoke's unbroken wreath,
Mounting in the windless air,
Rests, dissolving slowly there,
O'er the housetops like a cloud,
Or a thinnest vaporous shroud.

Morn has been—and lo! how soon
Has arrived the middle noon,
And the broad sun's rays do rest
On some naked mountain's breast,

Where alone relieve the eye
Massive shadows, as they lie
In the hollows motionless;
Still our boat doth onward press:
Now a peaceful current wide
Bears it on an ample tide;
Now the hills retire, and then
Their broad fronts advance again,
Till the rocks have closed us round,
And would seem our course to bound,
But anon a path appears,
And our vessel onward steers,
Darting rapidly between
Narrow walls of a ravine.

Morn has been and noon—and now
Evening falls about our prow:
'Mid the clouds that kindling won
Light and fire from him, the Sun
For a moment's space was lying,
Phœnix in his own flames dying!
And a sunken splendor still
Burns behind the western hill:
Lo! the starry troop again
Gather on the ethereal plain;
Even now and there were none,
And a moment since but one;

And anon we lift our head,
And all heaven is overspread
With a still-assembling crowd,
With a silent multitude—
Venus, first and brightest set
In the night's pale coronet,
Armed Orion's belted pride,
And the Seven that by the side
Of the Titan nightly weave
Dances in the mystic eve,
Sisters linked in love and light.
'Twere in truth a solemn sight,
Were we sailing now as they,
Who upon their western way
To the isles of spice and gold,
Nightly watching, might behold
These our constellations dip,
And the great sign of the Ship
Rise upon the other hand,
With the Cross, still seen to stand
In the vault of heaven upright,
At the middle hour of night—
Or with them whose keels first prest
The huge rivers of the West,
Who the first with bold intent
Down the Orellana went,*

* See Garcilasso's Conquest of Peru.

Or a dangerous progress won
On the mighty Amazon,
By whose ocean-streams they told
Of the warrior-maidens bold.

But the Fancy may not roam;
Thou wilt keep it nearer home,
Friend, of earthly friends the best,
Who on this fair river's breast
Sailest with me fleet and fast,
As the unremitting blast
With a steady breath and strong
Urges our light boat along.
We this day have found delight
In each pleasant sound and sight
Of this river bright and fair,
And in things which flowing are
Like a stream, yet without blame
These my passing song may claim;
Or thy hearing may beguile,
If we not forget the while,
That we are from childhood's morn
On a mightier river borne,
Which is rolling evermore
To a sea without a shore:
Life the river, and the sea
That we seek—eternity.

We may sometimes sport and play,
And in thought keep holyday,
So we ever own a law,
Living in habitual awe,
And beneath the constant stress
Of a solemn thoughtfulness—
Weighing whither this life tends,
For what high and holy ends
It was lent us, whence it flows,
And its current whither goes.

There is ample matter here
For as much of thought and fear
As will solemnize our souls—
Thought of how this river rolls
Over millions wrecked before
They could reach that happy shore,
Where we have not anchored yet;
Of the dangers which beset
Our own way—of hidden shoal,
Waters smoothest where they roll
Over point of sunken rock,
Treacherous calm, and sudden shock
Of the storm, which can assail
No boat than ours more weak or frail—
Matter not alone of sadness,
But no less of thankful gladness,

That, whichever way we turn,
There are steady lights that burn
On the shore, and lamps of love
In the gloomiest sky above,
Which will guide our bark aright
Through the darkness of our night—
Many a fixed, unblinking star
Unto them that wandering are
Through this blindly-weltering sea—
Themes of high and thoughtful glee,
When we think we are not left,
Of all solaces bereft,
Each to hold, companionless,
Through a watery wilderness,
Unaccompanied our way,
As we can: this I may say,
Whatsoever else betide,
With thee sitting at my side,
And this happy cherub sweet,
Playing, laughing, at my feet.

ON THE PERSEUS AND MEDUSA

OF BENVENUTO CELLINI, AT FLORENCE.

IN what fierce spasms upgathered, on the plain
Medusa's headless corpse has quivering sunk,
While all the limbs of that undying trunk
To their extremest joint with torture strain;
But the calm visage has resumed again
Its beauty—the orbed eyelids are let down,
As though a living sleep might once more crown
Their placid circlets, guiltless of all pain.
And thou—is thine the spirit's swift recoil,
Which follows every deed of acted wrath,
That holding in thy hand this lovely spoil,
Thou dost not triumph, feeling that the breath
Of life is sacred, whether it in form
Loathly or beauteous, man or beast or worm?

LINES

WRITTEN AT THE VILLAGE OF PASSIGNANO, ON THE LAKE OF THRASYMENE.

THE mountains stand about the quiet lake,
That not a breath its azure calm may break;
No leaf of these sere olive-trees is stirred,
In the near silence far-off sounds are heard;
The tiny bat is flitting overhead;
The hawthorn doth its richest odors shed
Into the dewy air; and over all,
Veil after veil, the evening shadows fall,
Withdrawing one by one each glimmering height,
The far, and then the nearer, from our sight—
No sign surviving in this tranquil scene,
That strife and savage tumult here have been.

But if the pilgrim to the latest plain
Of carnage, where the blood like summer rain
Fell but the other day—if in his mind
He marvels much and oftentimes to find
With what success has Nature each sad trace
Of man's red footmarks labored to efface—

What wonder, if this spot we tread appears
Guiltless of strife, when now two thousand years
Of daily reparation have gone by,
Since it resumed its own tranquillity?
This calm has nothing strange, yet not the less
This holy evening's solemn quietness,
The perfect beauty of this windless lake,
This stillness which no harsher murmurs break
Than the frogs croaking from the distant sedge,
These vineyards dressed unto the water's edge,
This hind that homeward driving the slow steer
Tells how man's daily work goes forward here,
Have each a power upon me, while I drink
The influence of the placid time, and think
How gladly that sweet Mother once again
Resumes her sceptre and benignant reign,
But for a few short instants scared away
By the mad game, the cruel, impious fray
Of her distempered children—how comes back,
And leads them in the customary track
Of blessing once again; to order brings
Anew the dislocated frame of things,
And covers up, and out of sight conceals
What they have wrought of ill, or gently heals.

VESUVIUS.

(AS SEEN FROM CAPRI.)

A WREATH of light-blue vapor, pure and rare,
Mounts, scarcely seen against the bluer sky,
In quiet adoration, silently—
Till the faint currents of the upper air
Dislimn it, and it forms, dissolving there,
The dome, as of a palace, hung on high
Over the mountain; underneath it lie
Vineyards, and bays, and cities, white and fair.
Might we not think this beauty would engage
All living things unto one pure delight?
Oh, vain belief!—for here, our records tell,
Rome's understanding tyrant from men's sight
Hid, as within a guilty citadel,
The shame of his dishonorable age.

VESUVIUS.

AS when unto a mother, having chid
Her child in anger, there have straight ensued
Repentings for her quick and angry mood,
Till she would fain see all its traces hid
Quite out of sight—even so has Nature bid
Fair flowers, that on the scarred earth she has strewed,
To blossom, and called up the taller wood
To cover what she ruined and undid.
Oh! and her mood of anger did not last
More than an instant, but her work of peace,
Restoring and repairing, comforting
The Earth, her stricken child, will never cease;
For that was her strange work, and quickly past,
To this her genial toil no end the years shall bring.

THE SAME,

CONTINUED.

THAT her destroying fury was with noise
And sudden uproar; but far otherwise,
With silent and with secret ministries,
Her skill of renovation she employs:
For Nature, only loud when she destroys,
Is silent when she fashions: she will crowd
The work of her destruction, transient, loud,
Into an hour, and then long peace enjoys.
Yea, every power that fashions and upholds,
Works silently — all things, whose life is sure,
Their life is calm; silent the light that moulds
And colors all things; and without debate
The stars, which are for ever to endure,
Assume their thrones and their unquestioned state.

LINES

WRITTEN AFTER HEARING SOME BEAUTIFUL SINGING IN A CONVENT-CHURCH AT ROME.

SWEET voices! seldom mortal ear
Strains of such potency might hear;
My soul, that listened, seemed quite gone,
Dissolved in sweetness, and anon
I was borne upward, till I trod
Among the hierarchy of God.
And when they ceased, as time must bring
An end to every sweetest thing,
With what reluctancy came back
My spirits to their wonted track,
And how I loathed the common life—
The daily and recurring strife
With petty sins, the lowly road,
And being's ordinary load!
—Why, after such a solemn mood,
Should any meaner thought intrude?
Why will not Heaven hereafter give,
That we for evermore may live

Thus at our spirit's topmost bent?
So asked I in my discontent.

But give me, Lord, a wiser heart;
These seasons come, and they depart—
These seasons, and those higher still,
When we are given to have our fill
Of strength, and life, and joy, with thee,
And brightness of thy face to see!
They come, or we could never guess
Of heaven's sublimer blessedness;
They come, to be our strength and cheer
In other times, in doubt or fear,
Or should our solitary way
Lie through the desert many a day.
They go—they leave us blank and dead,
That we may learn, when they are fled,
We are but vapors which have won
A moment's brightness from the sun,
And which it may at pleasure fill
With splendor, or unclothe at will.
Well for us they do not abide,
Or we should lose ourselves in pride,
And be as angels—but as they
Who on the battlements of day
Walked, gazing on their power and might,
Till they grew giddy in their height.

Then welcome every nobler time,
When out of reach of earth's dull chime
'Tis ours to drink with purgèd ears
The music of the solemn spheres,
Or in the desert to have sight
Of those enchanted cities bright,
Which sensual eye can never see:
Thrice welcome may such seasons be;
But welcome too the common way,
The lowly duties of the day,
And all which makes and keeps us low,
Which teaches us ourselves to know,
That we who do our lineage high
Draw from beyond the starry sky,
Are yet upon the other side—
To earth and to its dust allied.

ON A PICTURE OF THE ASSUMPTION,

BY MURILLO.

WITH what calm power thou risest on the wind—
Mak'st thou a pinion of those locks unshorn?
Or of that dark-blue robe which floats behind
In ample folds? or art thou cloud-upborne?

A crescent moon is bent beneath thy feet,
Above the heavens expand, and tier o'er tier
With heavenly garlands thy advance to greet,
The cloudy throng of cherubim appear.

There is a glory round thee, and mine eyes
Are dazzled, for I know not whence it came,
Since never in the light of western skies
The island-clouds burned with so pure a flame:

Nor were those flowers of our dull, common mould,
But nurtured on some amaranthine bed,
Nearer the sun, remote from storms and cold,
By purer dews and warmer breezes fed.

4*

Well may we be perplexed and sadly wrought,
That we can guess so ill what dreams were thine,
Ere from the chambers of thy silent thought
That face looked out on thee, painter divine!

What innocence, what love, what loveliness,
What purity, must have familiar been
Unto thy soul, before it could express
The holy beauty in that visage seen!

And so, if we would understand thee right,
And the diviner portion of thine art,
We must exalt our spirits to thy height,
Nor wilt thou else the mystery impart.

RECOLLECTIONS OF BURGOS.

MOST like some agèd king it seemed to me,
Who had survived his old regality,
Poor and deposed, but keeping still his state,
In all he had before of truly great;
With no vain wishes and no vain regret,
But his enforcèd leisure soothing yet
With meditation calm, and books, and prayer,
For all was sober and majestic there—
The old Castilian, with close finger-tips
Pressing his folded mantle to his lips;
The dim cathedral's cross-surmounted pile,
With carved recess, and cool and shadowy aisle;
The walks of poplar by the river's side,
That wound by many a straggling channel wide;
And seats of stone, where one might sit and weave
Visions, till well-nigh tempted to believe
That life had few things better to be done,
And many worse, than sitting in the sun
To lose the hours, and wilfully to dim
Our half-shut eyes, and veil them till might swim

The pageant by us, smoothly as the stream
And unremembered pageant of a dream.

A castle crowned a neighboring hillock's crest,
But now the moat was level with the rest;
And all was fallen of this place of power,
All heaped with formless stone, save one round tower,
And here and there a gateway low and old,
Figured with antique shape of warrior bold.
And then behind this eminence the sun
Would drop serenely, long ere day was done;
And one who climbed that height might see again
A second setting o'er the fertile plain
Beyond the town, and, glittering in his beam,
Wind far away that poplar-skirted stream.

GIBRALTAR.

ENGLAND, we love thee better than we know—
And this I learned, when, after wanderings long
'Mid people of another stock and tongue,
I heard again thy martial music blow,
And saw thy gallant children to and fro
Pace, keeping ward at one of those huge gates,
Which, like twin-giants, watch the Herculean straits:
When first I came in sight of that brave show,
It made my very heart within me dance,
To think that thou thy proud foot shouldst advance
Forward so far into the mighty sea;
Joy was it and exultation to behold
Thine ancient standard's rich emblazonry,
A glorious picture by the wind unrolled.

LINES,

SUGGESTED BY A PICTURE OF THE ADORATION OF THE MAGIANS.

LITTLE pomp or earthly state
On his lowly steps might wait;
Few the homages and small,
That the guilty earth at all
Was permitted to accord
To her King, and hidden Lord:
Therefore do we set more store
On these few, and prize them more:
Dear to us for this account
Is the glory of the Mount,
When bright beams of light did spring
Through the sackcloth covering—
Rays of glory forced their way
Through the garment of decay,
With which, as with a cloak, he had
His divinest splendor clad:
Dear the lavish ointment shed
On his feet and sacred head;

And the high-raised hopes sublime,
And the triumph of the time,
When through Zion's streets the way
Of her peaceful Conqueror lay,
Who, fulfilling ancient fame,
Meek and with salvation came.

But of all this scanty state
That upon his steps might wait,
Dearest are those Magian kings,
With their far-brought offerings.
From what region of the morn
Are ye come, thus travel-worn,
With those boxes pearl-embost,
Caskets rare, and gifts of cost?
While your swart attendants wait
At the stable's outer gate,
And the camels lift their head
High above the lowly shed;
Or are seen, a long-drawn train,
Winding down into the plain,
From beyond the light-blue line
Of the hills in distance fine.
Dear for your own sake, whence are ye?
Dearer for the mystery
That is round you—on what skies
Gazing, saw you first arise
Through the darkness that clear star,
Which has marshalled you so far,

Even unto this strawy tent—
Dancing up the Orient?*
Shall we name you kings indeed,
Or is this our idle creed?—
Kings of Seba, with the gold
And the incense long foretold?
Would the Gentile world by you
First-fruits pay of tribute due?
Or have Israel's scattered race,
From their unknown hiding-place,
Sent to claim their part and right
In the child new-born to-night?

But although we may not guess
Of your lineage, not the less
We the self-same gifts would bring,
For a spiritual offering.
May the frankincense, in air
As it climbs, instruct our prayer,
That it ever upward tend,
Ever struggle to ascend,
Leaving earth, yet ere it go
Fragrance rich diffuse below.
As the myrrh is bitter-sweet,
So in us may such things meet,

* "A star comes dancing up the Orient,
That springs for joy over the strawy tent."
G. Fletcher.

As unto the mortal taste
Bitter seeming, yet at last
Shall to them who try be known
To have sweetness of their own—
Tears for sin, which sweeter far
Than the world's mad laughters are;
Desires, that in their dying give
Pain, but die that we may live.
And the gold from Araby—
Fitter symbol who could see
Of the love which, thrice refined,
Love to God and to our kind,
Duly tendered, he will call
Choicest sacrifice of all?

Thus so soon as far apart
From the proud world, in our heart,
As in stable dark defiled,
There is born the Eternal Child,
May to him the spirit's kings
Yield their choicest offerings;
May the Affections, Reason, Will,
Wait upon him to fulfil
His behests, and early pay
Homage to his natal day.

SONNET.

IN A PASS OF BAVARIA BETWEEN THE WALCHEN AND THE WALDENSEE.

"His voice was as the sound of many waters."

A SOUND of many waters!—now I know
To what was likened the large utterance sent
By Him who 'mid the golden lampads went:
Innumerable streams, above, below,
Some seen, some heard alone, with headlong flow
Come rushing; some with smooth and sheer descent,
Some dashed to foam and whiteness, but all blent
Into one mighty music. As I go,
The tumult of a boundless gladness fills
My bosom, and my spirit leaps and sings:
Sounds and sights are there of the ancient hills,
The eagle's cry, or when the mountain flings
Mists from its brow, but none of all these things
Like the one voice of multitudinous rills.

SONNET.

RETURNING HOME.

TO leave unseen so many a glorious sight,
To leave so many lands unvisited,
To leave so many worthiest books unread,
Unrealized so many visions bright;—
Oh! wretched yet inevitable spite
Of our short span, and we must yield our breath,
And wrap us in the lazy coil of death,
So much remaining of unproved delight.
But hush, my soul, and vain regrets, be stilled!
Find rest in Him who is the complement
Of whatsoe'er transcends your mortal doom,
Of broken hope and frustrated intent;
In the clear vision and aspèct of whom
All wishes and all longings are fulfilled.

LINES,

WRITTEN IN AN INN.

A DREARY lot is his who roams
"Homeless among a thousand homes;"
A dreary thing it is to stray,
As I have sometimes heard men say,
And of myself have partly known,
A passing stranger and alone
In some great city: harder there,
With life about us everywhere,
Than in the desert to restrain
A sense of solitary pain.
We wander through the busy street,
And think how every one we meet
Has parents, sister, friend, or wife,
With whom to share the load of life;
We wander on, for little care
Have we to turn our footsteps there,
Where we are but a nameless guest,
One who may claim no interest

In any heart—a passing face,
That comes and goes, and leaves no trace;
Where service waits us, prompt but cold—
A loveless service, bought and sold.

Yet hard it is not to sustain
A time like this, if there remain
True greetings for us, hand and heart,
Wherein we claim the chiefest part,
Although divided now they be
By many a tract of land and sea.
If we can fly to thoughts like these,
Fall back on such sure sympathies,
This were sufficient to repress
That transient sense of loneliness.

Yet better, if, where'er we roam,
Another country, truer home,
Is in our hearts; if there we find
The word of power, that from the mind
All sad and drear thoughts shall repel,
All solitary broodings quell;
If in the joy of heaven we live,
Nor only on what earth can give,
Though pure and high—so we may learn
Unto the soul's great good to turn
What things soever best engage
Our thoughts towàrd our pilgrimage,

Which teach us this is not our rest,
That here we are but as a guest;
As doubtless 'twas no other thought
That in his holy bosom wrought,
Who not alone content to win
In life the shelter of an inn,
Was fain to finish the last stage
There of his mortal pilgrimage.*

We too, if we are wise, may be
Pleased for a season to be free
From the encumbrances which love—
Affection hallowed from above,
But earthly yet—has power to fling
About the spirit's heavenward wing;
Pleased if we feel that God is nigh,
Both where we live and where we die,
Whether among true kindred thrown,
Or seeming outwardly alone—
That, whether this or that befall,
He watches and has care of all.

* "He [Archbishop Leighton] used often to say, that, if he were to choose a place to die in, it should be an inn. It looks like a pilgrim's going home, to whom this world was all as an inn, and who was weary of the noise and confusion in it. He added that the officious care and tenderness of friends was an entanglement to a dying man, and that the unconcerned attendance of those that could be procured in such a place would give less disturbance; and he obtained what he desired."—*Burnet's History of his own Time.*

TO A LADY SINGING.

I.

HOW like a swan, cleaving the azure sky,
The voice upsoars of thy triumphant song,
That, whirled awhile resistlessly along
By the great sweep of threatening harmony,
Seemed, overmatched, to struggle helplessly
With that impetuous music; yet ere long
Escaping from the current fierce and strong,
Pierces the clear crystalline vault on high!
And I too am upborne with thee together
In circles ever narrowing, round and round,
Over the clouds and sunshine—who erewhile,
Like a blest bird of charmèd summer weather
In the blue shadow of some foamless isle,
Was floating on the billows of sweet sound.

II.

When the mute voice returns from whence it came,
The silence of a momentary awe,

A brief submission to the eternal law
Of beauty, doth to every heart proclaim
A Spirit has been summoned; yea, the same
Whose dwelling is the inmost human heart,
Which will not from that home and haunt depart—
Which nothing can quite vanquish or make tame.
It is the noblest gift beneath the moon,
The power this awful presence to compel
Out of the lurking-places where it lies
Deep-hidden and removed from human eyes:
Oh! reverence thou in fear and cherish well
This privilege of few—this rarest boon.

III.

Look! for a season (ah, too brief a space),
While yet the spell is strong upon the rout:
With something of still fear all move about,
As though a breath or motion might displace
The Spirit, which had come of heavenly grace
Among them, for a moment to redeem
Their thoughts and passions from the selfish dream
Of earthly life, and its inglorious race.
If we might keep this awe upon us still,
If we might walk for ever in the power
And in the shadow of the mystery,
Which has been spread around us at this hour,
This might suffice to guard us from much ill,
This might go far to keep us pure and free.

IV.

But the spell fails—and of the many here,
Who have been won to brief forgetfulness
Of all that would degrade them and oppress,
Who have been carried out of their dim sphere
Of being, to realms brighter and more clear,
How few to-morrow will retain a trace,
Which the world's business shall not soon efface,
Of this high mood, this time of reverent fear!
In these high raptures there is nothing sure,
Nothing that we can rest on, to sustain
The spirit long, or arm it to endure
Against temptation, weariness, or pain;
And if they promise to preserve it pure
From earthly taint, the promise is in vain.

V.

Yet proof is here of men's unquenched desire
That the procession of their life might be
More equable, majestic, pure, and free;
That there are times when all would fain aspire,
And gladly use the helps, to lift them higher,
Which music, poesy, or Nature brings,
And think to mount upon these waxen wings,
Not deeming that their strength shall ever tire.
But who indeed shall his high flights sustain,
Who soar aloft and sink not? He alone

Who has laid hold upon that golden chain
Of love, fast linked to God's eternal throne—
The golden chain from heaven to earth let down,
That we might rise by it, nor fear to sink again.

LINES.

NOT Thou from us, O Lord, but we
Withdraw ourselves from thee.

When we are dark and dead,
And thou art covered with a cloud,
Hanging before thee, like a shroud,
So that our prayer can find no way,
Oh! teach us that we do not say,
"Where is *thy* brightness fled?"

But that we search and try
What in ourselves has wrought this blame;
For thou remainest still the same,
But earth's own vapors earth may fill
With darkness and thick clouds, while still
The sun is in the sky.

THE ISLAND OF MADEIRA.

THOUGH never axe until a later day
    Assailed thy forests' huge antiquity,
Yet elder Fame had many tales of thee—
Whether Phœnician shipman far astray
Had brought uncertain notices away
Of islands dreaming in the middle sea;
Or that man's heart, which struggles to be free
From the old worn-out world, had never stay
Till, for a place to rest on, it had found
A region out of ken—that happier isle,
Which the mild ocean-breezes blow around—
Where they who thrice upon this mortal stage
Had kept their hands from wrong, their hearts from guile,
Should come at length, and live a tearless age.

ODE TO SLEEP.*

I.

I CAN NOT veil mine eyelids from the light;
I can not turn away
From this insulting and importunate day
That momently grows fiercer and more bright,
And wakes the hideous hum of monstrous flies
In my vexed ear, and beats
On the broad panes, and like a furnace heats
The chamber of my rest, and bids me rise.

II.

I can not follow thy departing track,
Nor tell in what far meadows, gentle Sleep,
Thou art delaying. I would win thee back,

* This and several succeeding poems were written many years ago. I mention this here, and indeed only mention it at all, because in a few places there are expressions occasionally of states of mind, in which I would not now ask others to sympathize, and from which I am thankful myself to have been delivered.

Were mine some drowsy potion, or dull spell,
Or charmèd girdle, mighty to compel
Thy heavy grace; for I have heard it said
Thou art no flatterer, that dost only keep
In kingly haunts, leaving unvisited
The poor man's lowlier shed;
And when the day is joyless, and its task
Unprofitable, I were fain to ask,
Why thou wilt give it such an ample space,
Why thou wilt leave us such a weary scope
For memory, and for that which men call hope.
Nor wind in one embrace
Sad eve, and night forlorn,
And undelightful morn.

III.

If with the joyous were thine only home,
I would not so far wrong thee as to ask
This boon, or summon thee from happier task.
But no—for then thou wouldst too often roam,
And find no rest; for me, I can not tell
What tearless lids there are, where thou mightst dwell:
I know not any, unenthralled of sorrow—
I know not one, to whom this joyous morrow,
So full of living motion new and bright,
Will be a summons to secure delight.
And thus I shall not harm thee, though I claim
Awhile thy presence.—O mysterious Sleep,

Some call thee shadow of a mightier Name,
And whisper how that nightly thou dost keep
A roll and count for him.—
Then be thou on my spirit like his presence dim!

IV.

Yet if my limbs were heavy with sweet toil,
I had not needed to have wooed thy might,
But till thy timely flight
Had lain securely in thy peaceful coil;
Or if my heart were lighter, long ago
Had crushed the dewy morn upon the sod,
Darkening where I trod,
As was my pleasure once, but now it is not so.

V.

And therefore am I seeking to entwine
A coronal of poppies for my head,
Or wreathe it with a wreath engarlanded
By Lethe's slumberous waters. Oh! that mine
Were some dim chamber turning to the north,
With latticed casement, bedded deep in leaves,
That opening with sweet murmur might look forth
On quiet fields from broad, o'erhanging eaves,
And ever when the Spring her garland weaves,
Were darkened with encroaching ivy-trail
And jaggèd vine-leaves' shade;
And all its pavement starred with blossoms pale

Of jasmine, when the wind's least stir was made;
Where the sunbeam were verdurous-cool, before
It wound into that quiet nook, to paint
With interspace of light and color faint
That tesselated floor.

VI.

How pleasant were it there in dim recess,
In some close-curtained haunt of quietness,
To hear no tones of human pain and care,
Our own or others'—little heeding there,
If morn, or noon, or night,
Pursued their weary flight,
But musing what an easy thing it were
To mix our opiates in a larger cup,
And drink, and not perceive
Sleep deepening lead his truer kinsman up,
Like undistinguished Night, darkening the skirts of Eve.

ATLANTIS.

I.

I COULD lose my boat,
And could bid it float
Where the idlest wind could pilot,
So its glad course lay
From this earth away,
Toward any untrodden islet.

II.

For this earth is old,
And its heart is cold,
And the palsy of age has bound it;
And my spirit frets
For the viewless nets
Which are hourly clinging round it.

III.

And with joyful glee
We have heard of thee,
Thou Isle in mid-ocean sleeping;
And thy records old,
Which the Sage has told
How the Memphian tombs are keeping.

IV.

But we know not where,
'Neath the desert air,
To look for the pleasant places
Of the youth of Time,
Whose austerer prime
The haunts of his childhood effaces.

V.

Like the golden flowers
Of the western bowers,
Have waned their immortal shadows;
And no harp may tell
Where the asphodel
Clad in light those Elysian meadows.

VI.

And thou, fairest Isle
In the daylight's smile,
Hast thou sunk in the boiling ocean,
While beyond thy strand
Rose a mightier land
From the wave in alternate motion?

VII.

Are the isles that stud
The Atlantic flood,
But the peaks of thy tallest mountains—
While repose below
The great waters' flow
Thy towns and thy towers and fountains?

VIII.

Have the Ocean powers
Made their quiet bowers
In thy fanes and thy dim recesses?
Or in haunts of thine
Do the sea-maids twine
Coral-wreaths for their dewy tresses?

IX.

Or does foot not fall
In deserted hall,
Choked with wrecks that ne'er won their haven,
By the ebb trailed o'er
Thy untrampled floor,
Which their sunken wealth has paven?

X.

Oh, appear! appear!—
Not as when thy spear
Ruled as far as the broad Ægean,
But in Love's own might,
And in Freedom's right,
Till the nations uplift their Pæan—

XI.

Who now watch and weep,
And their vigil keep,
Till they faint for expectation;
Till their dim eyes shape
Temple, tower, and cape,
From the cloud and the exhalation.

SAIS.

AN awful statue, by a veil half hid,
At Sais stands. One came, to whom was known
All lore committed to Etruscan stone,
And all sweet voices, that dull Time has chid
To silence now, by antique Pyramid,
Skirting the desert, heard; and what the deep
May in its dimly-lighted chambers keep,
Where Genii groan beneath the seal-bound lid.
He dared to raise that yet unlifted veil
With hands not pure, but never might unfold
What there he saw: madness, the shadow, fell
On his few days, ere yet he went to dwell
With Night's eternal people, and his tale
Has thus remained, and will remain, untold.

SONNET.

I STOOD beside a pool, from whence ascended,
Mounting the cloudy platforms of the wind,
A stately hern — its soaring I attended,
Till it grew dim, and I with watching blind —
When, lo! a shaft of arrowy light descended
Upon its darkness and its dim attire:
It straightway kindled then, and was afire,
And with the unconsuming radiance blended.
A bird, a cloud, flecking the sunny air,
It had its golden dwelling 'mid the lightning
Of those empyreal domes, and it might there
Have dwelt for ever, glorified and bright'ning,
But that its wings were weak — so it became
A dusky speck again, that *was* a wingèd flame.

THE CONSTITUTIONAL EXILES OF 1823.

[WRITTEN IN 1829.]

WISE are ye in a wisdom vainly sought
Through all the records of the historic page;
It is not to be learned by lengthened age,
Scarce by deep musings of unaided thought:
By suffering and endurance ye have bought
A knowledge of the thousand links that bind
The highest with the lowest of our kind,
And how the indissoluble chain is wrought.
Ye fell by your own mercy once:—beware,
When your lots leap again from Fortune's urn,
A heavier error—to be pardoned less!
Yours be it to the nations to declare
That years of pain and disappointment turn
Weak hearts to gall, but wise to gentleness.

TO THE SAME.

LIKE nightly watchers from a palace-tower,
 In hope, and faith, and patience strong, to wait
The beacons on the hills, which should relate
How some fenced city of deceit and power
Had fallen—ye have stood for many an hour,
Till your first hope's high movements must be dead;
And if with new ye have not cheered and fed
Your bosoms, dim despair may be your dower.
Yet not for all—though yet no fire may crest
The mountains, or light up their beacons sere—
Your eminent commission so far wrong,
Or so much flatter the oppressors' rest,
As to give o'er your watching; for so long
As ye shall hope, 'tis reason they must fear.

THE KINGDOM OF GOD.

I SAY to thee, do thou repeat
To the first man thou mayest meet
In lane, highway, or open street—

That he, and we, and all men, move
Under a canopy of love,
As broad as the blue sky above:

That doubt and trouble, fear and pain
And anguish, all are shadows vain;
That death itself shall not remain:

That weary deserts we may tread,
A dreary labyrinth may thread,
Through dark ways underground be led:

Yet, if we will one Guide obey,
The dreariest path, the darkest way,
Shall issue out in heavenly day.

And we, on divers shores now cast,
Shall meet, our perilous voyage past,
All in our Father's house at last.

And ere thou leave him, say thou this,
Yet one word more: they only miss
The winning of that final bliss—

Who will not count it true that Love,
Blessing, not cursing, rules above,
And that in it we live and move.

And one thing further make him know—
That to believe these things are so,
This firm faith never to forego—

Despite of all which seems at strife
With blessing, all with curses rife—
That this *is* blessing, this *is* life.

I.

SOME murmur when their sky is clear,
  And wholly bright to view,
If one small speck of dark appear
  In their great heaven of blue.
And some with thankful love are filled,
  If but one streak of light,
One ray of God's good mercy, gild
  The darkness of their night.

II.

In palaces are hearts that ask,
  In discontent and pride,
Why life is such a dreary task,
  And all good things denied.
And hearts in poorest huts admire
  How love has in their aid
(Love that not ever seems to tire)
  Such rich provision made.

ON AN EARLY DEATH.

I.

AH me! of them from whom the good have hope,
Of them whom Virtue for her liegemen claims,
How many the world tames,
That with its evil they quite cease to cope,
And their first fealty sworn to beauty and truth
Break early; and amid their sinful youth
Make shipwreck of all high and glorious aims!
How few the fierce and fiery trial stand,
To be as weapons tempered and approved
For an Almighty hand!
How few of all the streamlets that were moved,
Do ever unto clearness run again!
And therefore is it marvellous to us,
When of these weapons one is broken thus,
When of these fountains one would seem in vain
Renewed in clearness, and is stanched before
It has had leave to spread fresh streams the desert o'er.

II.

Ah me! that by so frail and feeble thread
Our life is holden—that not life alone,

But all that life has won,
May in an hour be gathered to the dead;
The slow additions that build up the mind,
The skill that by temptation we have bought
And suffering, and whatever has been taught
By lengthened years and converse with our kind,
That all may cease together—and the tree
Reared to its height by many a slow degree,
And by the dews, the sunshine, and the showers,
Of many springs, an instant may lay low,
With all its living towers,
And all the fruit mature of growth and slow,
Which on the trees of wisdom leisurely must grow.

III.

Alas! it is another thing to wail,
That when the foremost runners sink and fail,
They can not pass their torch or forward place
To them that are behind them in the race,
But their extinguished torches must be laid
Together with them in the dust of death:
That when the wise and the true-hearted fade,
So little of themselves they can bequeath
To us, who yet are in the race of life,
For labor and for toil, for weariness and strife.

IV.

—But from behind the veil,
Where they are entered who have gone before,

A solemn voice arrests my feeble wail:—
"And has thy life such worthier aims, O man,
That thou shouldst grudge to give its little span
To truth and knowledge, and faith's holy lore.
Because the places for the exercise
Of these may be withdrawn from mortal eyes?
Win truth, win goodness—for which man was made—
And fear not thou of these to be bereft,
Fear not that these shall in the dust be laid,
Or in corruption left,
Or be the grave-worm's food.
Nothing is left or lost—nothing of good,
Or lovely; but whatever its first springs
Has drawn from God, returns to him again;
That only which 'twere misery to retain
Is taken from you, which to keep were loss;
Only the scum, the refuse, and the dross,
Are borne away unto the grave of things:
Meanwhile, whatever gifts from Heaven descend,
Thither again have flowed,
To the receptacle of all things good,
From whom they come and unto whom they tend,
Who is the First and Last, the Author and the End.

V.

"And fear to sorrow with increase of grief,
When they who go before
Go furnished—or because their span was brief,

When in the acquist of what is life's true gage,
Truth, knowledge, and that other worthiest lore,
They had fulfilled already a long age.
For doubt not but that in the worlds above
There must be other offices of love;
That other tasks and ministries there are,
Since it is promised that His servants, there
Shall serve Him still. Therefore be strong, be strong,
Ye that remain, nor fruitlessly revolve,
Darkling, the riddles which ye can not solve,
But do the works that unto you belong;
Believing that for every mystery,
For all the death, the darkness, and the curse,
Of this dim universe,
Needs a solution full of love must be:
And that the way whereby ye may attain
Nearest to this, is not through broodings vain
And half-rebellious—questionings of God,
But by a patient seeking to fulfil
The purpose of his everlasting will,
Treading the path which lowly men have trod.
Since it is ever they who are too proud
For this, that are the foremost and most loud
To judge his hidden judgments—these are still
The most perplexed and lost at his mysterious will."

FROM THE PERSIAN.

DEATH ends well Life's undelight,
Yet Life shudders at Death's sight.

Life the dark hand sees, but not
What it brings, the clear cup bright.

So at sight of Love a heart
Fears that it must perish quite.

Only Self, the tyrant dark,
He must perish in Love's might—

That the heart may truly live,
Breathing free in Love's pure light.

XERXES AT THE HELLESPONT.

[SUGGESTED BY A POEM IN KNAPP'S GEDICHTE.]

"CALM is now that stormy water—it has learned to fear my wrath:
Lashed and fettered, now it yields me for my hosts an easy path!"
Seven long days did Persia's monarch on the Hellespontine shore,
Throned in state, behold his armies without pause defiling o'er;
Only on the eighth the rearward to the other side were past—
Then one haughty glance of triumph far as eye could reach he cast:
Far as eye could reach he saw them, multitudes equipped for war—
Medians with their bows and quivers, linkèd armor and tiar:
From beneath the sun of Afric, from the snowy hills of Thrace,
And from India's utmost borders, nations gathered in one place:

At a single mortal's bidding all this pomp of war unfurled—
All in league against the freedom and the one hope of the world!

"What though once some petty trophies from my captains thou hast won,
Think not, Greece, to see another such a day as Marathon:
Wilt thou dare await the conflict, or in battle hope to stand,
When the lord of sixty nations takes himself his cause in hand?
Lo! they come, and mighty rivers, which they drink of once, are dried;
And the wealthiest cities beggared, that for them one meal provide.
Powers of number by their numbers infinite are overborne,
So I measure men by measure, as a husbandman his corn.
Mine are all—this sceptre sways them—mine is all in every part!"
And he named himself most happy, and he blessed himself in heart—
Blessed himself, but on that blessing tears abundant followed straight,
For that moment thoughts came o'er him of man's painful brief estate:

Ere a hundred years were finished, where would all those myriads be?
Hellespont would still be rolling his blue waters to the sea;
But of all those countless numbers, not one living would be found—
A dead host with their dead monarch, silent in the silent ground.

HARMOSAN.

[SEE GIBBON'S "DECLINE AND FALL," C. 51.]

I.

NOW the third and fatal conflict for the Persian throne was done,
And the Moslem's fiery valor had the crowning victory won.

II.

Harmosan, the last and boldest the invader to defy,
Captive overborne by numbers, they were bringing forth to die.

III.

Then exclaimed that noble captive: "Lo I perish in my thirst;
Give me but one drink of water, and let then arrive the worst!"

IV.

In his hand he took the goblet, but awhile the draught forbore,
Seeming doubtfully the purpose of the foemen to explore.

V.

Well might then have paused the bravest—for around
him angry foes
With a hedge of naked weapons did that lonely man
enclose.

VI.

"But what fear'st thou?" cried the Caliph;—"is it,
friend, a secret blow?
Fear it not!—our gallant Moslem no such treacherous
dealing know.

VII.

"Thou mayst quench thy thirst securely, for thou shalt
not die before
Thou hast drunk that cup of water—this reprieve is
thine—no more!"

VIII.

Quick the Satrap dashed the goblet down to earth with
ready hand,
And the liquid sank for ever, lost amid the burning
sand.

IX.

"Thou hast said that mine my life is, till the water of
that cup
I have drained: then bid thy servants that spilled water
gather up!"

X.

For a moment stood the Caliph as by doubtful passions stirred—
Then exclaimed: "For ever sacred must remain a monarch's word.

XI.

"Bring another cup, and straightway to the noble Persian give:
Drink, I said before, and perish—now I bid thee drink and live!"

GERTRUDE OF SAXONY.

I.

A CLOUDY pillar before Israel went,
An angel kept Tobias in the way,
A star led up the Magians to the tent,
Wherein new-born the Child of Glory lay.
Therefore the wayfarers will always say:—
"Praise be to Him who guides his servants' feet,
Who keeps them that no evil may assay
To do them harm—when storm or hot rays beat,
A refuge from the storm, a shadow from the heat."

II.

On Saxon soil her journey had begun,
A gentle pilgrim on a holy quest,
Nor will she that long journey's end have won
Until Alsatian soil her feet have prest:
This maiden there would be a convent's guest,
Whereof the glory far and wide is told,
And there she would take up her lasting rest;
For there, while love of many has grown cold,
The earnest discipline of ancient times they hold.

III.

And others in her company there were,
An agèd kinsman—and, intent on gain,
Some merchants with them the same way did fare;
Till once when night o'ertook them in the plain,
No shelter won, the merchants then were fain
Re-seek their lodging lately left behind:
The holy pilgrims might not so restrain
Their eager steps, but trusted well to find,
Ere night was fully come, some shelter to their mind.

IV.

But sooner than they looked for, thickest night
Fell—and they gazed around them, if perchance
The lowliest cottage might appear in sight,
For now return they could not, nor advance:
When of a sudden, on that plain's expanse,
A palace of surpassing beauty rare
Seemed to stand up before them at a glance.
Then gladly did they thitherward repair,
Hoping to find due rest and needful succor there.

V.

And being there arrived, they marvelled much,
For doors and windows open wide they found,
And all without doors and within was such,
With such perfection of fresh beauty crowned,

As though in that day's space from out the ground
New-risen.—Entering in, they wondering saw
How all things for life's use did there abound,
But inmate none appearing, they for awe
And secret fear well-nigh were tempted to withdraw.

VI.

But when they for a season waited had,
Behold! a Matron of majestic air,
Of regal port, in regal garments clad,
Entered alone—who, when they would declare,
With reverence meet, what need had brought them there
At such untimely hour, smiling replied,
That she already was of all aware;
And added, she was pleased and satisfied
That they to be her guests that night had turned aside.

VII.

And ere the meal she spread for them was done,
Upon a sudden One there entered there,
Whose countenance with marvellous beauty shone,
More than the sons of men divinely fair,
And all whose presence did the likeness wear
Of angel more than man: he too, with bland,
Mild words saluted them, and gracious air;
Sweet comfort, solemn awe, went hand in hand,
While in his presence did those wondering pilgrims stand.

VIII.

Then turning to that Matron, as a son
Might to a mother speak familiarly,
He spake to her—they only heard the tone,
Not listening, out of reverent courtesy:
And then with smile of large benignity
Saluting them again, he left the place,
And was not more seen by them—only she,
That Matron, stayed and talked with them a space,
Whose words were full of sweetness and of heavenly grace

IX.

And then she showed them chambers for their rest,
And did not that tired maiden then forget
To take, and lead apart, her weary guest;
And pointing where a ready couch was set,
She with her own hands spread the coverlet
Above her, bidding her till morning rose
That she should render unto Sleep his debt,
And suffer him her heavy lids to close;
Then, with a blessing given, she left them to repose.

X.

The morning come, she bade them rise anon,
For now their fellow-travellers were in sight,
Journeying that way, and would be quickly gone—
The merchants whom they quitted yesternight.

Refreshed they rose to meet the early light,
And to rejoin their company prepared:
But first due thanks they tendered, as was right,
To her who had for them so amply cared:
And with those thankful hearts forth on their way they fared.

XI.

So they set forward from that stately hall,
And now had journeyed for a little space,
When musing much and wondering much at all
Which had befallen them there, they turned their face
Its fair proportions once again to trace—
When lo! with newer awe their hearts were filled:
For it had wholly vanished from its place,
Like some cloud-palace that the strong winds build,
Which to unmake again they presently have willed.

XII.

While this new admiration them did seize,
They saw some nobles of the land that way
Come riding.—Straightway they inquired of these,
If they had never seen, nor yet heard say,
Of some great dome that in that quarter lay.
But these to them made answer constantly,
How they had ridden past by night and day,
But that such stately hall might nowhere be—
Only the level plain, such as they now might see.

XIII.

Thereat from them did thankful utterance break,
And with one voice they praised His tender care
Who had upreared a palace for their sake,
And of that pomp and cost did nothing spare,
Though but to guard them from one night's cold air—
And had no ministries of love disdained:
And 'twas their thought, if some have unaware
Angels for guests received with love unfeigned,
That they had been by more than angels entertained.

TO ——.

WE live not in our moments or our years:
The present we fling from us like the rind
Of some sweet future, which we after find
Bitter to taste, or bind *that* in with fears,
And water it beforehand with our tears—
Vain tears for that which never may arrive:
Meanwhile the joy whereby we ought to live,
Neglected, or unheeded, disappears.
Wiser it were to welcome and make ours
Whate'er of good, though small, the present brings—
Kind greetings, sunshine, song of birds, and flowers,
With a child's pure delight in little things;
And of the griefs unborn to rest secure,
Knowing that mercy ever will endure.

TO THE EVENING STAR.

SOLE star that glitterest in the crimson west,
"Fair child of beauty, glorious lamp of Love,
How cheerfully thou lookest from above"—
With what unblinking eye and jocund crest!
Yet grief from thee has passed into my breast,
For all-surpassing glory needs must be
Full unto us of sad perplexity
Seen from this place of sin and sin's unrest.
Yea, all things which such perfect beauty own
As this of thine is, tempt us unto tears;
For whether thou sole-sittest on thy throne,
Or leadest choral dances of thy peers,
Thou and all Nature, saving man alone,
Fulfil with music sweet your Maker's ears.

SONNET.

ALL beautiful things bring sadness, nor alone
Music, whereof that wisest poet spake;*
Because in us keen longings they awake
After the good for which we pine and groan,
From which exiled we make continual moan,
Till once again we may our spirits slake
At those clear streams, which man did first forsake,
When he would dig for fountains of his own.
All beauty makes us sad, yet not in vain—
For who would be ungracious to refuse,
Or not to use, this sadness without pain,
Whether it flows upon us from the hues
Of sunset, from the time of stars and dews,
From the clear sky, or waters pure of stain?

* "I am never merry when I hear sweet music."
SHAKESPEARE.

LORD, what a change within us one short hour
Spent in thy presence will prevail to make—
What heavy burdens from our bosoms take,
What parchèd grounds refresh, as with a shower!
We kneel, and all around us seems to lower;
We rise, and all, the distant and the near,
Stands forth in sunny outline, brave and clear;
We kneel how weak, we rise how full of power!
Why, therefore, should we do ourselves this wrong,
Or others—that we are not always strong;
That we are ever overborne with care;
That we should ever weak or heartless be,
Anxious or troubled, when with us in prayer,
And joy, and strength, and courage, are with thee?

A GARDEN so well watered before morn
Is hotly up, that not the swart sun's blaze,
Down-beating with unmitigated rays,
Nor arid winds from scorching places borne,
Shall quite prevail to make it bare and shorn
Of its green beauty—shall not quite prevail
That all its morning freshness shall exhale,
Till evening and the evening dews return—
A blessing such as this our hearts might reap,
The freshness of the garden they might share,
Through the long day a heavenly freshness keep,
If, knowing how the day and the day's glare
Must beat upon them, we would largely steep
And water them betimes with dews of prayer.

WHEN hearts are full of yearning tenderness,
For the loved absent, whom we can not reach—
By deed or token, gesture or kind speech,
The spirit's true affection to express;
When hearts are full of innermost distress,
And we are doomed to stand inactive by,
Watching the soul's or body's agony,
Which human effort helps not to make less—
Then like a cup capacious to contain
The overflowings of the heart, is prayer:
The longing of the soul is satisfied,
The keenest darts of anguish blunted are;
And, though we can not cease to yearn or grieve,
Yet we have learned in patience to abide.

I.

THIS did not once so trouble me,
    That better I could not love Thee;
    But now I feel and know
That only when we love, we find
How far our hearts remain behind
    The love they should bestow.

II.

While we had little care to call
On thee, and scarcely prayed at all,
    We seemed enough to pray:
But now we only think with shame,
How seldom to thy glorious Name
    Our lips their offerings pay.

III.

And when we gave yet slighter heed
Unto our brother's suffering need,
    Our hearts reproached us then
Not half so much as now, that we
With such a careless eye can see
    The woes and wants of men.

IV.

In doing is this knowledge won,
To see what yet remains undone;
    With this our pride repress,
And give us grace, a growing store,
That day by day we may do more,
    And may esteem it less.

LORD, many times I am aweary quite
Of mine own self, my sin, my vanity—
Yet be not thou, or I am lost outright,
Weary of me.

And hate against myself I often bear,
And enter with myself in fierce debate:
Take thou my part against myself, nor share
In that just hate!

Best friends might loathe us, if what things perverse
We know of our own selves, they also knew:
Lord, Holy One! if thou who knowest worse
Shouldst loathe us too!

THE DAY OF DEATH.

THOU inevitable day,
When a voice to me shall say—
"Thou must rise and come away:

"All thine other journeys past,
Gird thee, and make ready fast
For thy longest and thy last"—

Day deep-hidden from our sight
In impenetrable night,
Who may guess of thee aright?

Art thou distant, art thou near?
Wilt thou seem more dark or clear?
Day with more of hope or fear?

Wilt thou come, not seen before
Thou art standing at the door,
Saying, light and life are o'er?

Or with such a gradual pace,
As shall leave me largest space
To regard thee face to face?

Shall I lay my drooping head
On some loved lap? round my bed
Prayer be made and tears be shed?

Or at distance from mine own,
Name and kin alike unknown,
Make my solitary moan?

Will there yet be things to leave,
Hearts to which this heart must cleave,
From which parting it must grieve?

Or shall life's best ties be o'er,
And all loved ones gone before
To that other happier shore?

Shall I gently fall on sleep—
Death, like slumber, o'er me creep,
Like a slumber sweet and deep?

Or the soul long strive in vain
To get free, with toil and pain
From its half-divided chain?

Little skills it where or how,
If thou comest then or now—
With a smooth or angry brow:

Come thou must, and we must die—
Jesus, Savior, stand thou by,
When that last sleep seals our eye!

TO A FRIEND.

THE courses of our lives, that side by side
Ran for some little while, are sundered now;
We meet not now, as once, day after day,
In pleasant intercourse to 'change our thoughts:
Yet I remember often all that time,
And all the thoughts that filled it—for just then
We were as merchants seeking goodly pearls,
Seeking one pearl of price; and when we read
In books of some, or met on life's highway,
Who had returned as from a fruitless quest,
Bringing these tidings only, that all lands
They had gone through, had searched the farthest coasts,
Wherever Fame reported that such pearl
Was to be won, but still had nothing found,
And now believed not there was aught to find,
Our hearts would die within us, loath to leave
Their hope, which yet grew weaker day by day,
That somewhere was a key which should unlock
The many chambers of this human life,
A law harmoniously to reconcile

All the perplexèd appearances of things,
A treasure which should make the finder rich
For ever: for slight profit then to us,
And little comfort might we draw from things
Wherein some found, or thought at least they found,
The immortal longings of their spirits slaked,
And all life's mystery lightened. What at best
The beautiful creations of man's art,
If resting not on some diviner ground
Than man's own mind that formed them—at the best
What but the singing of a mournful dirge,
What but the scattering flowers upon the grave
Of man's abandoned hopes and buried joys?
Oh, miserable comfort! Loss is loss,
And death is death; and after all is done—
After the flowers are scattered on the tomb,
After the singing of the sweetest dirge—
The mourner, with his heart uncomforted,
Returning to his solitary home,
Thinks with himself, if any one had aught
Of stronger consolation, he should speak;
If not, 'twere best for ever to hold peace,
And not to mock him with vain words like these.
Such, and no more—to us contemplating
The life of man—such, and no truer, seemed
The alleviations to be won from these—
Poor, withering garlands flung upon a grave,
The mournful beauty of a couchant Sphinx,

Watching by some half-buried pyramid,
Or fallen column in the wilderness!

And Nature's self, our foster-mother dear,
What could she do for us? what help impart?
Or when we felt that we were orphans here,
Or when our orphan hearts within us mourned,
And fled unto her bosom, there to find
Pity and love, there were no beatings there,
There were no pulses in her cold, cold heart;
She had no happy family of love,
In which to adopt us. Beauty without love,
How should it cherish or make less forlorn
The forlorn heart of man? what comfort yield?
Yea, rather must it be a tearful thing,
And such we felt it; such it was to us,
Who gazed upon the incense-breathing flowers,
Trees and rejoicing rivers—sun and stars,
Keeping their courses in untroubled joy,
By sin unstained, by longings undisturbed,
While we, the first-fruits of creation—we
For whose dear sake all other things were made—
Were as we were: but they appeared to us
Like the hired servants whom the Prodigal
Bethought him of, as satisfied with bread;
While we, the children of our Father's house,
Were perishing with hunger far away.
What longing had we then to be as these,

To be as flowers or trees, as rocks or stones!
Glad might we have relinquished and put by
The burden of our immortality,
And all the drear prerogatives of man.

Or sometimes finding little nearer home,
That we should love to dwell with our own hearts,
We looked abroad, and spake of some bright dawn
Of happiness and freedom, peace and love,
Day long desired, and now about to break
On all the nations—yet the while we felt
That we were speaking false and hollow words—
For how should man, despairing of himself,
Have hope for others?—where no centre is—
Centre established sure of life and joy—
What is it but an idle thing to draw
The widest circle of imagined good
At distance round us?—where 'tis ill with each,
How vain to hope it should be well with all!

But now, though not to outward change we look
For the fulfilling of that glorious hope,
Have we renounced that hope—? or is it grown
A less substantial vision, because now
No fabled world, imagined isles beyond
The limitary ocean, such as never
Have been but in the longing of man's heart,
Not these now occupy our hearts and hopes;

But Eden and the New Jerusalem,
The garden and the city of our God,
The things which have been and shall be again,
Fill up the prospect upon either side,
Before us and behind? or have we left
Our love for Nature, now to love her less,
Since we have learned that all we so admire
Is yet but as her soiled and weekday dress,
And nothing to the glory she shall wear,
When for the coming sabbath of the world
She shall put on her festival attire—
Or closed our hearts to what of beautiful
Man by strong spell and earnest toil has won
To take intelligible forms of art,
Now that all these are recognised to be
Desires and yearnings, feeling after him
And by him only to be satisfied,
Who is himself the eternal Loveliness?

Has it been so with us, that men should say,
That they should say with reason, we have now
Narrowed our hearts, forsaken our old joy
In Nature, or renounced the glorious hope
That once we cherished for the race of man?
That hope, that joy, that longing, still are ours,
And shall continue with us to the end,
Else better not to be. True is it, we walk
Under the shadow of such mysteries,

That how should they not darken us sometimes?
And how in such a mournful world as this,
Should Love be other than a sorrowing thing—
A call to grieve? for though its golden key
Sets open to us a new world of joys,
Yet has it griefs and sorrows of its own,
Making things grievous that we once could bear
To look at with a careless, tearless eye.

TO POETRY.

I.

IN my life's youth, while yet the deeper needs
Of the inmost spirit unawakened were,
Thou couldst recount of high, heroic deeds,
Couldst add a glory unto earth and air—
A crowning glory, making fair more fair:
So that my soul was pleased and satisfied,
Which had as yet no higher, deeper care,
And said that thou shouldst evermore abide
With me, and make my bliss, and be my spirit's bride.

II.

But years went on, and thoughts which slept before,
Over the horizon of my soul arose—
Thoughts which perplexed me ever more and more;
As though a Sphinx should meet one, and propose
Enigmas hard, and which whoso not knows
To interpret, must her prey and victim be;
And I, round whom thick darkness seemed to close,
Knew only this one thing, that misery
Remained, if none could solve this riddle unto me.

III.

Then I remembered how from thy lips fell
Large words of promise, how thou couldst succeed
All darkest mysteries of life to spell;
Therefore I pleaded with thee now to read
The riddle that was baffling me, with speed,
To yield some answer to the questioning.
Something thou spak'st, but nothing to my need,
So that I counted thee an idle thing,
Who, having promised much, couldst no true succor bring.

IV.

And I turned from thee, and I left thee quite,
And of thy name to hear had little care:
For I was only seeking if by flight
I might shun *her*, who else would rend and tear
Me, who could not her riddle dark declare:—
This toil, the anguish of this flight, was mine,
Until at last, inquiring everywhere,
I won an answer from another shrine,
A holier oracle, a temple more divine.

V.

But when no longer without hope I mourned,
When peace and joy revived in me anew,
Even from that moment my old love returned,
My former love, yet wiser and more true,

As seeing what for us thy power can do,
And what thy skill can make us understand
And know—and where that skill attained not to;
How far thou canst sustain us by thy hand,
And what things shall in us a holier care demand—

VI.

My love of thee and thine—for earth and air,
And every common sight of sea and plain,
Then put new robes of glory on, and wear
The same till now, and things which dead had lain
Revived, as flowers that smell the dew and rain:
I was a man again of hopes and fears;
The fountains of my heart flowed forth again,
Whose sources had seemed dry for many years,
And there was given me back the sacred gift of tears.

VII.

And that old hope, which never quite had perished,
A longing which had stirred me from a boy,
And which in darkest seasons I had cherished—
Which nothing could quite vanquish or destroy—
This, with all other things of life and joy,
Revived within me—and I too would seek
The power, that moved my own heart, to employ
On others, who perchance would hear me speak,
If but the tones were true, although the voice were weak.

VIII.

Though now there seems one only worthy aim
For poet—that my strength were as my will!—
And which renounce he can not without blame—
To make men feel the presence by his skill
Of an eternal loveliness, until
All souls are faint with longing for their home,
Yet the same while are strengthened to fulfil
Their work on earth, that they may surely come
Unto the land of Life, who here as exiles roam.

IX.

And what though loftiest fancies are not mine,
Nor words of chiefest power, yet unto me
Some voices reach out of the inner shrine,
Heard in my heart of hearts, and I can see
At times some glimpses of the majesty,
Some prints and footsteps of the glory trace,
Which have been left on earth, that we might be
By them led forward to the secret place,
Where we perchance might see that glory face to face.

X.

If in this quest, O power of sacred song,
Thou canst assist—oh, never take thy flight!
If thou canst make us gladder or more strong,
If thou canst fling glimpses of glorious light

Upon life's deepest depth and highest height,
Or pour upon its low and level plain
A gleam of mellower gladness, if this might
Thou hast — (and it is thine) — then not in vain
Are we henceforth prepared to follow in thy train.

SONNET.

WHAT is thy worship but a vain pretence,
Spirit of Beauty, and a servile trade,
A poor and an unworthy traffic made
With the most sacred gifts of soul and sense—
If they who tend thine altars, gathering thence
No strength, no purity, may still remain
Selfish and dark, and from life's sordid stain
Find in their ministrations no defence?
—Thus many times I ask, when aught of mean
Or sensual has been brought unto mine ear,
Of them whose calling high is to insphere
Eternal Beauty in forms of human art—
Vexed that my soul should ever moved have been
By that which has such feigning at the heart!

POEMS

FROM

EASTERN SOURCES.

NOTE.

The following Poems bear somewhat a vague title, because such only would accurately suit compositions which have been derived in very different degrees from the sources thus indicated. Some are mere translations; others have been modelled anew, and only such portions used of the originals as were adapted to my purpose; of others it is only the imagery and thought which are Eastern, and these have been put together in new combinations; while of others it is the hint, and nothing more, which has been borrowed — it may be from some prose source. On this subject, however, more information will be given in the notices which precede several of the poems.

ALEXANDER AT THE GATES OF PARADISE.

A Legend from the Talmud.

SEE Eisenmenger's "*Entdecktes Judenthum,*" v. ii., p. 321, with whom I trust that my readers will not agree, for he has scarcely patience to finish this "*narrische Talmudische Fabel,*" as he styles it. It reappears, slightly modified, in the Persian tradition, according to which, Alexander, having conquered the world, determined to seek out the fountain of life and immortality. In like manner, in the Christian poems of the middle ages, Alexander is made to recognise at last the vanity and emptiness of all the glory which he has won, and is hardly turned from his purpose of going forth at last in search of the lost Paradise: see Rosenkranz' "*Gesch. d. Deutschen Poesie in Mittelalter,*" p. 367. Very notable is this making Alexander, and no other, the man from whom the confession comes, that the world has not that which can truly satisfy man's spirit, but that he still yearns for something beyond. It is like, in Scripture, the same confession coming from the lips of Solomon; for in each case the experiment has been made under the most favorable circumstances: so that, in one case, as in the other, it may be asked, "What can the man do, that cometh after the king?" (Eccles. ii. 12.)

FIERCE was the glare of Cashmere's middle day,
When Alexander for Hydaspes bent,
Through trackless wilds urged his impetuous way:

Who yet in that wide, wasteful continent
A little valley found, so calm, so sweet,
He there awhile to tarry was content.

A crystal stream was murmuring at his feet,
Whereof the monarch, when his meal was done,
Took a long draught, to slake his fever heat.

Again he drank, and yet again, as one
Who would have drained that fountain crystalline
Of all its waves, and left it dry anon:

For in his veins, ofttimes a fire with wine,
And in his bosom, throne of sleepless pride,
The while he drank, went circling peace divine.

It seemed as though all evil passions died
Within him, slaked was every fire accurst;
So that in rapturous joy aloud he cried:—

"Oh! might I find where these pure waters first
Shoot sparkling from their living fountain-head—
Oh, there to quench my spirit's inmost thirst!

"Sure, if we followed where these waters led,
We should at length some fairer region gain
Than yet has quaked beneath our iron tread—

"Some land that should in very truth contain
Whate'er we dream of beautiful and bright,
And idly dreaming of, pursue in vain!

"That land must stoop beneath our conquering might.
Companions dear, this toil remains alone,
To win that region of unmatched delight.

"O faithful in a thousand labors known,
One toil remains, the noblest and the last;
Let us arise, and make that land our own!"

—Through realms of darkness, wildernesses vast,
All populous with sights and sounds of fear,
In heat and cold, by day and night, he past—

With trumpet-clang, with banner, and with spear;
Yearning to drink that river, where it sent
Its first pure waters forth, serene and clear:

Till boldest captains sank, their courage spent,
And dying cried, "This stream all search defies!"
But never would he tarry nor repent—

Nor pitched his banners, till before his eyes
Rose high as heaven, in its secluded state
The mighty, verdant wall of Paradise.

And lo! that stream, which early still and late
He had tracked upward, issued bright and clear
From underneath the angel-guarded gate.

—"And who art thou that has adventured here,
Daring to startle this serene abode
With flash of mortal weapons, sword and spear?"

So the angelic sentinel of God,
Fire-flashing, to the bold invader cried,
Whose feet profane those holy precincts trod.

The son of Philip without dread replied:—
"Is Alexander's fame unknown to thee,
Which the world knows—mine, who have victory tied

"To my sword's hilt, and who, while stoop to me
All other lands, would win what rich or fair
This land contains, and have it mine in fee?"

—"Thou dost thyself proclaim that part or share
Thou hast not here. O man of blood and sin,
Go back!—with those blood-stainèd hands despair

"This place of love and holy peace to win:
This is the gate of righteousness, and they,
The righteous, only here may enter in."

Around, before him, lightnings dart and play:
He undismayed—"Of travail long and hard
At least some trophy let me bear away."

—"Lo! then this skull—which, if thou wilt regard,
And to my question seek the fit reply,
All thy long labors shall have full reward.

"Once in that hollow circle lodged an eye,
That was, like thine, for ever coveting—
Which worlds on worlds had failed to satisfy.

"Now, while thou gazest on that ghastly ring,
From whence of old a greedy eye outspied,
Say thou what was it—for there was a thing—

"Which filled at last and thoroughly satisfied
The eye that in that hollow circle dwelt,
So that, 'Enough, I have enough,' it cried."

—Blank disappointment at the gift he felt,
And, hardly taking, turned in scorn away;
Nor he the riddle of the angel spelt—

But cried unto his captains: "We delay,
And at these portals lose our time in vain,
By more than mortal terrors kept at bay:

"Come—other lands as goodly spoils contain;
Come—all too long untouched the Indian gold,
The pearls and spice of Araby, remain!—

"Come, and who will this riddle may unfold."
Then stood before him, careless of his ire,
An Indian sage, who rendered answer bold:—

"Lord of the world, commanded to inquire
What was it that could satisfy an eye,
That organ of man's measureless desire—

"By deed and word *thou* plainly dost reply,
That its desire can nothing tame or quell,
That it can never know sufficiency.

"While thou enlargest thy desire as hell,
Filling thy hand, but filling not thy lust,
Thou dost proclaim man's eye insatiable:

"Such answer from thy lips were only just.
Yet 'twas not so. One came at last, who threw
Into yon face a heap of vilest dust—

"Whereof a few small grains did fall into
And filled the orb and hollow of that eye;
When that which suffisance not ever knew
Before, was fain, 'I have enough,' to cry."

CHIDHER'S WELL.

Of Chidher's Well, the Eastern *λουτρὸν παλιγγενεσίας*, Von Hammer, in the very interesting introduction to his "History of Persian Poetry," gives a good account. Among other things, he says: "Contemporary with Moses lived the Prophet Chiser, of whom some hold that he is the same with Elias, while others altogether distinguish them. He is one of the chief personages of Eastern mythology, the ever-ready helper of the oppressed, the Genius of Spring, the deliverer in peril, the admonisher of princes, the avenger of unrighteousness, the guide through the wilderness of the world, and, finally, the ever-youthful guardian of the fountain of life. As such he revives the youth of men, and beasts, and plants, gives back lost beauty, and in spring arrays the dead earth with its fresh garments of green. His fountain bestows on whosoever drinks it eternal beauty, youth, and wisdom. What wonder, then, that all mortals with burning desire seek it, though as yet not one — not even Alexander, the conqueror of the world, who, in quest of it, undertook an expedition into the land of darkness — has found it!" Probably this, his journey through the land of darkness, is but a mythic form of his expedition through the Libyan desert to the temple of Jupiter Ammon.

Of this poem I may observe that it is the first of several in the volume written with an arrangement of rhyme hardly familiar to the English reader, which yet is that of a great part, as I believe, of the lyric poetry of the East, and which may not, perhaps, be unworthy of a place among us. According to the laws of the Ghazel — for poems in this metre are so entitled — the first two lines must rhyme, and then this rhyme repeats itself in the second line of each succeeding couplet, which is, in fact, a new stanza, till the end of the poem — the termination of the first line in each of these following couplets being left free. This single rule of the one repeated rhyme being observed, the Ghazel admits otherwise of the greatest possible variety: it may be composed, as is this present, in short trochaics, in longer or shorter iambics, or, in fact, in lines of whatsoever length or arrangement of syllables the poet will. In Germany, the Ghazel has been perfectly domesticated. Rückert and Count Platen are, I believe, considered to have cultivated it with the greatest success.

I.

THEE have thousands sought in vain
Over land and barren main—

II.

Chidher's well—of which men say,
That thou makest young again;

III.

Fountain of eternal youth,
Washing free from every stain.

IV.

To thy waves the agèd moons
Aye betake them, when they wane;

V.

And the suns their golden light,
While they bathe in thee, retain.

VI.

From that fountain drops are flung,
Mingling with the vernal rain,

VII.

And the old earth clothes itself
In its young attire again.

VIII.

Thitherward the freckled trout
Up the water-courses strain,

IX.

And the timid, wild gazelles
Seek it through the desert plain.

X.

Great Iskander,* mighty lord,
Sought that fountain, but in vain;

XI.

Through the land of darkness went
In its quest with fruitless pain,

XII.

When by wealth of conquered worlds
Did his thirst unslaked remain.

XIII.

Many more with parchèd lip
Must lie down, and dizzy brain—

XIV.

And of that, a fountain sealed
Unto them, in death complain.

XV.

If its springs to thee are known,
Weary wanderer, tell me plain.

* Alexander.

XVI.

From beneath the throne of God
It must well, a lucid vein.

XVII.

To its sources lead me, Lord,
That I do not thirst again—

XVIII.

And my lips not any more
Shall the earth's dark waters stain.

THE BANISHED KINGS.

In the first edition of these Poems, I expressed myself unacquainted with the source from which this story was derived, and did not trace it up higher than Rückert's "*Bramanische Erzählungen,*" p. 5; on the model of whose poem my own, without pretending to be an accurate translation, was yet closely formed. It owns, I believe, a higher antiquity even than the beautiful Greek romance of the seventh or eighth century, "Barlaam and Josaphat," often ascribed, but on no sufficient grounds, to John of Damascus; but, at any rate, it is one of the many exquisite moral tales and apologues with which that work is adorned.

ON a fair ship, borne swiftly o'er the deep,
A man was lying, wrapped in dreamless sleep;
When unawares upon a sunken rock
The vessel struck, and shattered with the shock.
But strange! the plank where lay the sleeper bore
Him, wrapped in deep sleep ever, to the shore:
It bore him safely through the foam and spray,
High up on land, where couched 'mid flowers he lay.
Sweet tones first woke him from his sleep, when round
His couch observant multitudes he found:
All hailed him then, and did before him bow,
And with one voice exclaimed, "Our king art thou!"

With jubilant applause they bore him on,
And set him wondering on a royal throne:
And some his limbs with royal robes arrayed,
And some before him duteous homage paid,
And some brought gifts, all rare and costly things,
Nature's and Art's profusest offerings:
Around him counsellors and servants prest,
All eager to accomplish his behest.
Wish unaccomplished of his soul was none;
The thing that he commanded, it was done.

Much he rejoiced, and he had well-nigh now
Forgotten whence he hither came, and how:
Until at eve, of homage weary grown,
He craved a season to be left alone.
Alone in hall magnificent he sate,
And mused upon the wonder of his fate;
When lo! an agèd counsellor, a seer,
Before unnoticed, to the king drew near:
—"And thee would I too gratulate, my son,
Who hast thy reign in happy hour begun:
Seen hast thou the beginning—yet attend,
While I shall also show to thee the end.
That this new fortune do not blind thee quite,
Both sides regard, its darker as its bright:
Heed what so many, who have ruled before,
Failing to heed, now rue for evermore.
Though sure thy state and strong thy throne appear,
King only art thou for a season here;

A time is fixed, albeit unknown to thee,
Which, when it comes, thou banished hence shalt be.
Round this fair world, though hidden from the eye
By mist and vapor, many islands lie:
Bare are their coasts, and dreary and forlorn,
And unto them the banished kings are borne;
On each of these an exiled king doth mourn.
For when a new king comes, they bear away
The old, whom now no vassals more obey;
Stripped of his royalties and glories lent,
Unhonored and unwilling he is sent
Unto his dreary island banishment,
While all who girt his throne with service true,
Now fall away from him, to serve the new.
What I have told thee, lay betimes to heart,
And ere thy rule is ended, take thy part,
That thou hereafter on thine isle forlorn
Do not thy vanished kingdom vainly mourn,
When nothing of its pomp to thee remains
On that bare shore, save only memory's pains.

"Much, O my prince! my words have thee distrest,
Thy head has sunk in sorrow on thy breast;
Yet idle sorrow helps not—I will show
A nobler way, which shall true help bestow.
This counsel take—to others given in vain,
While no belief from them my words might gain.
Know, then, whilst thou art monarch here, there stand
Helps for the future many at command:

Then, while thou canst, employ them to adorn
That island whither thou must once be borne.
Unbuilt, and waste, and barren, now that strand;
There gush no fountains from the thirsty sand;
No groves of palm-trees have been planted there,
Nor plants of odorous scent embalm that air;
While all alike have shunned to contemplate
That they should ever change their flattering state.
But make thou there provision of delight,
Till that which now so threatens, may invite;
Bid there thy servants build up royal towers,
And change its barren sands to leafy bowers;
Bid fountains there be hewn, and cause to bloom
Immortal amaranths, shedding rich perfume.
So when the world, which speaks thee now so fair,
And flatters so, again shall strip thee bare,
And drive thee naked forth in harshest wise,
Thou joyfully wilt seek thy paradise.
There will not vex thee memories of the past,
While hope will heighten here the joys thou hast.
This do, while yet the power is in thy hand—
While thou hast helps so many at command."

Then raised the prince his head with courage new,
And what the sage advised, prepared to do.
He ruled his realm with meekness, and meanwhile
He marvellously decked the chosen isle;
Bade there his servants build up royal towers,
And change its barren sands to leafy bowers;

Bade fountains there be hewn, and caused to bloom
Immortal amaranths, shedding rich perfume.
And when he long enough had kept his throne,
To him sweet odors from that isle were blown:
Then knew he that its gardens blooming were,
And all the yearnings of his soul were there.
Grief was it not to him, but joy, when they
His crown and sceptre bade him quit one day:
When him his servants rudely did dismiss,
'Twas not the sentence of his ended bliss;
But pomp and power he cheerfully forsook,
And to his isle a willing journey took,
And found diviner pleasure on that shore,
Than all his proudest state had known before.

THE

BALLADS OF HAROUN AL RASCHID.

I.

THE SPILT PEARLS.

THOLUCK has translated this story in his "*Blüthensammlung aus der Morgenländischen Mystik,*" p. 339, from the "*Bustan*" of Saadi.

I.

HIS courtiers of the Caliph crave—
  "Oh, say how this may be,
That of thy slaves, this Ethiop slave
  Is best beloved by thee?

II.

"For he is hideous as the night:
  Yet when has ever chose
A nightingale for its delight
  A hueless, scentless rose?"

III.

The Caliph then—" No features fair
  Nor comely mien are his:
Love is the beauty he doth wear,
  And love his glory is.

IV.

" Once when a camel of my train
  There fell in narrow street,
From broken casket rolled amain
  Rich pearls before my feet.

V.

" I nodding to my slaves, that I
  Would freely give them these,
At once upon the spoil they fly,
  The costly boon to seize.

VI.

" One only at my side remained—
  Beside this Ethiop, none:
He, moveless as the steed he reined,
  Behind me sat alone.

VII.

" 'What will thy gain, good fellow, be,
  Thus lingering at my side?'—
—'My king, that I shall faithfully
  Have guarded thee,' he cried.

VIII.

"'True servant's title he may wear,
He only, who has not,
For his lord's gifts, how rich soe'er,
His lord himself forgot!'"

IX.

—So thou alone dost walk before
Thy God with perfect aim,
From him desiring nothing more
Beside himself to claim.

X.

For if thou not to him aspire,
But to his gifts alone,
Not love, but covetous desire,
Has brought thee to his throne.

XI.

While such thy prayer, it climbs above
In vain—the golden key
Of God's rich treasure-house of love,
Thine own will never be.

II.

THE BARMECIDES.

THE anecdote on which this poem is founded is related by Sylvestre de Sacy, in the "*Chrestomathie Arabe,*" v. ii. See also D'Herbelot's "*Bibliothèque Orientale,*" art. *Barmekian.*

HAROUN the Just!—yet once that name
Of Just the ruler ill became,
By whose too hasty sentence died
The royal-hearted Barmecide.
O Barmecide, of hand and heart
So prompt, so forward to impart,
Of bounty so unchecked and free,
That once a poet sung, how he
Would fear thy very hand to touch,
Lest he should learn to give too much,
Lest, catching the contagion thence
Of thy unmatched munificence,
A beggar he should soon remain,
Helpless his bounty to restrain—
O Barmecide, of royal heart,
My childhood's tears again will start
Into mine eyes—the tears I shed,
As I remember, when I read
Of harsh injustice done to thee,
And all thy princely family.

—What marvel that the Caliph, stung
With secret consciousness of wrong,
Or now desiring every trace
Of that large bounty to efface,
With penalty of death forbade
That mourning should for them be made;
That any should with grateful song
Their memory in men's hearts prolong?
—"And who art thou, that day by day
Hast dared my mandate disobey?
Who art thou whom my guards have found,
Now standing on some grass-grown mound,
Now wandering 'mid the ruined towers,
Fallen palaces, and wasted bowers,
Of those at length for traitors known,
And by my justice overthrown—
Singing a plaintive dirge for them
Whom my just vengeance did condemn;
Till ever, as I learn, around
Thy steps a listening crowd is found,
Who still unto thy sad lament
Do with their sobs and tears consent;
While in the bosom of that throng
Rise thoughts that do their monarch wrong?
What doom I did for this assign
Thou knewest, and that doom is thine!"

But then the offender: "Give me room,
And I will gladly take my doom.

O king, to spend my latest breath,
Ere I am borne unto my death,
In telling for what highest grace
I was beholden to that race,
Whose memory my heart hath kept,
Whose wasted glories I have wept.
For then, at least, it will appear
That not in disobedience mere
Thy mandate high I overpast.
—O king, I was the least and last
Of all the servitors of him,
Whose glory in thy frown grew dim—
The least and last—yet he one day
To me, his meanest slave, did say
That he was fain my guest to be,
And the next day would sup with me.
More time I willingly had craved,
But my excuses all he waved,
And by no train accompanied,
His two sons only at his side,
At my poor lodging lighted down,
Which at the limits of the town
Stood in a close and narrow street.
Him I and mine did humbly greet,
Standing before him while he shared
What we meanwhile had best prepared
Of entertainment, though the best
Was poor and mean for such a guest.

But supper done, with cheerful mien,
'Thy house,' he cried, 'I have not seen—
Thy gardens;—let me pace awhile,
Along some cool and shadowy aisle.'
I thought he mocked me, but replied:—
'Possessions have I not so wide;
For house, another room with this
Our only habitation is;
And garden have I none to show,
Unless that narrow court below,
Shut in with lofty walls, that name
In right of four dwarf shrubs may claim.'
—'Nay, nay,' he answered, 'there is more,
If only we could find the door.'
Again I told him, but in vain,
That he had seen my whole domain.
—'Nay, go then quick, a mason call.'
Him bade he straightway pierce the wall.
—'But shall we in this wise invade
A neighbor's house?'—No heed he paid,
And I stood dumb, and wondering
Whereto he would the issue bring.
Anon he through the opening past,
He and his sons, and I the last:
When suddenly myself I found
In ample space of garden-ground,
Or rather in a paradise
Of rare and wonderful device,

With stately walks and alleys wide,
Far stretching upon every side;
And streams, upon whose either bank
Stood lofty platanes, rank by rank,
And marble fountains, scattering high
Illumined dewdrops in the sky;
And making a low, tinkling sound,
As sliding down from mound to mound,
They did at last their courses take
Down to a calm and lucid lake,
By which, on gently-sloping height,
There stood a palace of delight;
And many slaves, but all of rare
And perfect beauty, marshalled there,
Did each to me incline the knee,
Exclaiming all, 'Thy servants we.'

"And then my lord cried laughing: 'Nay,
When this is thine, how couldst thou say
That thou hadst shown me all before?
Thine is it all.'—He said no more,
But at my benefactor's feet
I falling, thanks would render meet.
He scarcely listening, turned his head,
And to his eldest son he said:—
'This house, these gardens, 'twere in vain,
Unless enabled to maintain,
That he should call them his;—my son,
Let us not leave this grace half done.'

Who then replied: 'My farms beyond
The Tigris I by sealèd bond
This night, before we part, will see
Made over unto him in fee.'
—' 'Tis well; but there will months ensue,
Ere his incomings will be due.
What shall there, the meanwhile, be done?'
He turned unto his younger son,
Who answered: 'I will bid that gold,
Ten thousand pieces, shall be told
Unto his steward presently;
These shall his urgent needs supply.'
'Twas done upon that very eve;
And done, anon they took their leave,
And left me free to contemplate
The wonders of my novel state.

"Prince of the Faithful, mighty king,
My fortunes from this source had spring,
Which, if they since that time have grown,
Him their first author still they own.
Nor when that name, which *was* the praise
Of all the world, on evil days
Had fallen, was I content to let
Be quite forgotten the large debt
I owed to him—content to die,
If such shall be thy pleasure high,
And my offence shall seem to thee
Deserving of such penalty."

What marvel that the king who heard
Was in his inmost bosom stirred?
What marvel that he owned the force
Of late regret and vain remorse?
That spreading palm, whose boughs had made,
Far stretching, such an ample shade
For many a wanderer through life's waste,
He had hewn down in guilty haste;
That fountain free, that springing well
Of goodness inexhaustible,
His hand had stopped it, ne'er again
To slake the thirst of weary men;
That genial sun, which evermore
Did on a cold, chill world outpour
Its rays of love, and life, and light,
'T was he who quenched in darkest night!
What marvel that he owned the force
Of late regret and vain remorse,
And (all he could) now freely gave
The life the other did not crave?
Nay, more, the offender did dismiss
With gifts and praise; nor only this,
But did the unrighteous law reverse,
Which had forbidden to rehearse,
And in the minds of men prolong,
By grateful speech or plaintive song,
The bounteous acts and graces wide,
And goodness of the Barmecide.

III.

THE FESTIVAL.

SEE Sylvestre de Sacy's "*Chrestomathie Arabe,*" v. ii., p. 3.

I.

FIVE hundred princely guests before
Haroun Al Raschid sate;
Five hundred princely guests or more
Admired his royal state:

II.

For never had that glory been
So royally displayed,
Nor ever such a gorgeous scene
Had eye of man surveyed.

III.

He, most times meek of heart, yet now
Of spirit too elate,
Exclaimed: "Before me Cæsars bow,
On me two empires wait.

IV.

"Yet all our glories something lack,
We do our triumphs wrong,
Until to us reflected back
In mirrors clear of song.

V.

"Call him, then, unto whom this power
Is given—this skill sublime:
Now win from us some gorgeous dower
With song that fits the time."

VI.

—"My king, as I behold thee now,
May I behold thee still,
While prostrate worlds before thee bow,
And wait upon thy will!

VII.

"May evermore this clear, pure heaven,
Whence every speck and stain
Of trouble far away is driven,
Above thy head remain!"

VIII.

The Caliph cried: "Thou wishest well;
There waits thee golden store
For this—but, oh! resume the spell,
I fain would listen more."

IX.

—"Drink thou life's sweetest goblet up,
O king, and may its wine,
For others' lips a mingled cup,
Be all unmixed for thine!

X.

"Live long—the shadow of no grief
Come ever near to thee:
As thou in height of place art chief,
So chief in gladness be."

XI.

Haroun Al Raschid cried again:—
"I thank thee—but proceed,
And now take up a higher strain,
And win a higher meed."

XII.

Around that high, magnific hall,
One glance the poet threw
On courtiers, king, and festival,
And did the strain renew:—

XIII.

"And yet—and yet—shalt thou at last
Lie stretched on bed of death:
Then, when thou drawest thick and fast
With sobs thy painful breath—

XIV.

"When Azrael glides through guarded gate,
  Through hosts that camp around
Their lord in vain—and will not wait,
  When thou art sadly bound

XV.

"Unto thy house of dust alone,
  O king, when thou must die—
This pomp a shadow thou shalt own,
  This glory all a lie!"

XVI.

Then darkness on all faces hung,
  And through the banquet went
Low sounds the murmuring guests among
  Of angry discontent.

XVII.

And him anon they fiercely urge:—
  "What guerdon shall be thine?
What does it, this untimely dirge,
  'Mid feasts, and flowers, and wine?

XVIII.

"Our lord demanded in his mirth
  A strain to heighten glee;
But, lo! at thine his tears come forth
  In current swift and free."

XIX.

—"Peace! not to him rebukes belong,
But rather highest grace;
He gave me what I asked, a song
To fit the time and place."

XX.

All voices at that voice were stilled;
Again the Caliph cried:—
"He saw our mouths with laughter filled,
He saw us drunk with pride—

XXI.

"And bade us know that every road,
By monarch trod or slave,
Thick set with thorns, with roses strowed,
Doth issue in the grave."

THE SEASONS.

I.

WINTER.

I.

WHITE ermine now the mountains wear,
To shield their naked shoulders bare.

II.

The dark pine wears the snow, as head
Of Æthiop doth white turban wear.

III.

The floods are armed with silver shields,
Through which the Sun's sword can not fare:

IV.

For he who in the mid heaven rode,
In golden arms, on golden chair—

V.

Now through small corner of the sky
Creeps low, nor warms the foggy air.

VI.

To mutter 'twixt their teeth the streams,
In icy fetters, scarcely dare.

VII.

Hushed is the busy hum of life;
'Tis silence in the earth and air.

VIII.

From mountain issues the gaunt wolf,
And from its forest-depths the bear.

IX.

Where is the garden's beauty now?
The thorn is here; the rose, oh, where?

X.

The trees, like giant skeletons,
Wave high their fleshless arms and bare—

XI.

Or stand like wrestlers stripped and bold,
And strongest winds to battle dare.

XII.

It seems a thing impossible
That earth its glories should repair:

XIII.

That ever this bleak world again
Should bright and beauteous mantle wear—

XIV.

Or sounds of life again be heard
In this dull earth and vacant air.

II.

SPRING.

I.

WHO was it that so lately said,
All pulses in thy heart were dead—

II.

Old Earth, that now in festal robes
Appearest, as a bride new wed?

III.

Oh, wrapped so late in winding-sheet,
Thy winding-sheet, oh! where is fled?

IV.

Lo! 'tis an emerald carpet now,
Where the young monarch, Spring, may tread.

V.

He comes—and, a defeated king,
Old Winter, to the hills is fled.

VI.

The warm wind broke his frosty spear,
And loosed the helmet from his head:

VII.

And he weak showers of arrowy sleet
For his strongholds has vainly sped.

VIII.

All that was sleeping is awake,
And all is living that was dead.

IX.

Who listens now, can hear the streams
Leap tinkling down their pebbly bed—

X.

Or see them, from their fetters free,
Like silver snakes the meadows thread.

XI.

The joy, the life, the hope of earth,
They slept awhile, they were not dead:

XII.

O thou who say'st thy sere heart ne'er
With verdure can again be spread—

XIII.

O thou who mournest them that sleep,
Low lying in an earthy bed—

XIV.

Look out on this reviving world,
And be new hopes within thee bred!

III.

SUMMER.

I.

Now seems all Nature to conspire,
As to dissolve the world in fire—

II.

Which dies among its odorous sweets,
A Phœnix on its funeral-pyre.

III.

Simoom breathes hotly from the waste,
The green earth quits its green attire:

IV.

Floats o'er the plain the liquid heat,
Cheating the traveller's fond desire—

V.

Illusion fair of lake and stream,
Receding as he draweth nigher.

VI.

Ice is more precious now than gold,
Snow more than silver men desire.

VII.

'Tis far to seek unfailing wells
For tender maid or agèd sire:

VIII.

Men know the worth of water now,
And learn to prize God's blessing higher;

IX.

The shallow pools have disappeared,
Caked into iron is the mire.

X.

Through clouds of dust the crimson sun
Glares on the earth in lurid ire:

XI.

The parchèd earth with thirsty lips
Is gasping, ready to expire.

XII.

Oh, happy, who by liquid streams
In shady gardens can retire—

XIII.

Where murmuring falls and whispering trees
Sweet slumber to invite conspire:

XIV.

Or where he may deceive the time
With volume sage, or pensive lyre.

IV.

AUTUMN.

I.

THINE, Autumn, is unwelcome lore—
To tell the world its pomp is o'er:

II.

To whisper in the rose's ear,
That all her beauty is no more:

III.

And bid her own the faith how vain
Which Spring to her so lately swore.

IV.

A queen deposed, she quits her state;
The nightingales her fall deplore:

V.

The hundred-voicèd bird may woo
The thousand-leavèd flower no more.

VI.

The jasmine sinks its head in shame,
The sharp east wind its tresses shore:

VII.

And robbed in passing cruelly
The tulip of the crown it wore.

VIII.

The lily's sword is broken now,
That was so bright and keen before—

IX.

And not a blast can blow, but strews
With leaf of gold the earth's dank floor.

X.

The piping winds sing Nature's dirge,
As through the forest bleak they roar—

XI.

Whose leafy screen, like locks of eld,
Each day shows scantier than before.

XII.

Thou fadest as a flower, O man!
Of food for musing here is store.

XIII.

O man! thou fallest as a leaf:
Pace thoughtfully earth's leaf-strewn floor—

XIV.

Welcome the sadness of the time,
And lay to heart this natural lore.

PROVERBS,

TURKISH AND PERSIAN.

I.

SECTS seventy-two, they say, the world infest,
And each and all lie hidden in thy breast.

II.

Moses' one staff, so slight as it appears,
Aye breaks in shivers Pharaoh's thousand spears.

III.

Forget not Death, O man! for thou may'st be
Of one thing certain—he forgets not thee.

IV.

The world's a tavern, where to-night men swill:
To-morrow brings the headache and the bill.

V.

Speaks one of good which falls not to thy lot?
He also speaks of ill which thou hast not.

VI.

Boast not thy service rendered to the king;
'Tis grace enough he lets thee service bring.

VII.

Lies once thy cart in quagmire overthrown,
Thy path to thee by thousands will be shown.

VIII.

Oh, square thyself for use: a stone that may
Fit in the wall is left not in the way.

IX.

Never the game has happy issue won,
Which with the cotton has the fire begun.

X.

The sandal-tree, most sacred tree of all,
Perfumes the very axe which bids it fall.

XI.

Who doth the raven for a guide invite,
Must marvel not on carcases to light.

XII.

Each man has more of four things than he knows:
What four are these?—sins, debts, and years, and foes

XIII.

The king but with one apple maketh free,
And straight his servants have cut down the tree.

XIV.

Two friends will in a needle's eye repose,
But the whole world is narrow for two foes.

XV.

Rejoice not when thine enemy doth die—
Thou hast not won immortal life thereby.

XVI.

Be bold to bring forth fruit, though stick and stone
At the fruit-bearing trees are flung alone.

XVII.

This world is like a carcase in the way;
Who eagerly throng round it, dogs are they.

XVIII.

While in thy lips thy words thou dost confine,
Thou art their lord; once uttered, they are thine.

XIX.

Oh, seize the instant time; you never will
With waters once passed by impel the mill.

XX.

Boldly thy bread upon the waters throw,
And if the fishes do not, God will know.

XXI.

What will not time and toil?—by these a worm
Will into silk a mulberry-leaf transform.

XXII.

There is no ointment for the wolf's sore eyes
Like clouds of dust which from the sheep arise.

XXIII.

When what thou willest has befallen not, still
This help remains, what has befallen to will.

XXIV.

Inquire not if thy soul be foul or fair,
But if toward God its efforts striving are.

XXV.

The lily with ten tongues can hold its peace;
Wilt thou with one from babbling never cease?

XXVI.

How shall the praise of silence best be told?
To speak is silver, to hold peace is gold.

XXVII.

Thy word unspoken thou canst any day
Speak, but thy spoken ne'er again unsay.

XXVIII.

The world's great wheel in silence circles round,
A housewife's spindle with unceasing sound.

XXIX.

O babbler, couldst thou but the cause divine,
Why one tongue only, but two ears, are thine!

XXX.

What mystic roses in thy breast will blow,
If on the wind their leaves thou straightway strow!

THE FALCON.

I.

HIGH didst thou once in honor stand,
The falcon on a prince's hand:

II.

Thine eye, unhooded and unsealed,
All depths of being pierced and scanned:

III.

All worlds of space from end to end
Thy never-wearied pinion spanned.

IV.

O falcon of the spiritual heaven,
Entangled in an earthly band—

V.

While all too eagerly thy prey
Pursuing in a lower land—

VI.

In hope abide;—thy Monarch yet
For thy release shall give command—

VII.

And bid thee to resume again
Thy place upon thy Monarch's hand.

THE BREAKER OF IDOLS.

MAHMOUD, the great Mohammedan conqueror of India, reached, in his career of victory, Somnát, of which the gates have since become familiar to us — a temple of peculiar sanctity in the southern extremity of Guzerát. Having overcome all resistance, he entered the temple. "Facing the entrance was Somnát — an idol five yards high, of which two were buried in the ground. Mahmoud instantly ordered the image to be destroyed; when the Bramins of the temple threw themselves before him, and offered an enormous ransom if he would spare their deity. . . . . Mahmoud, after a moment's pause, declared that he would rather be remembered as the breaker than the seller of idols, and struck the image with his mace. His example was instantaneously followed; and the image, which was hollow, burst with the blows, and poured forth a quantity of diamonds and other jewels which amply repaid Mahmoud for the sacrifice of the ransom." — *Elphinstone's History of India,* v. i., p. 554.

LO! a hundred proud pagodas have the Moslem torches burned,
Lo! a thousand monstrous idols Mahmoud's zeal has overturned.

He from northern Ghuznee issuing, through the world one word doth bear: —
"God is ONE; ye shall no other with the peerless One compare!" —

Till in India's farthest corner he has reached the costliest shrine
Of the Bramins, idol-tending—which they hold the most divine.

Profits not the wild resistance; stands the victor at the gate,
With this hugest idol's ruin all his work to consummate.

Forth in long procession streaming came the suppliant priests to meet—
Came with ransom and with homage the resistless one to greet.

Ransom huge of gold they offer, pearls of price and jewels rare,
Purchase of their idol's safety, this their dearest will he spare.

And there wanted not who counselled that he should his hand withhold—
Should that single image suffer, and accept this needed gold.

But he rather—"God has raised me, not to make a shameful gain,
Trafficking in hideous idols with a service false and vain:

"But to count my work unfinished till I sweep them from the world:
Stand, and see the thing ye sued for, by this hand to ruin hurled!"

High he reared his battle-axe, and heavily came down
the blow:
Reeled the abominable image, broken, bursten, to and
fro—

From its shattered sides revealing pearls and diamonds,
showers of gold;
More than all that proffered ransom, more than all a
hundred-fold.

Thou, too, Heaven's commissioned warrior to cast down
each idol throne
In thy heart's profanèd temple, make this faithful deed
thine own.

Still they plead and still they promise, wilt thou suffer
them to stand;
They have pleasures, gifts, and treasures, to enrich thee
at command.

Heed not thou, but boldly strike them; let descend the
faithful blow:
From their wreck and from their ruin first will thy true
riches flow.

Thou shalt lose thy life, and find it; thou shalt boldly
cast it forth:
And then, back again receiving, know it in its endless
worth.

LIFE THROUGH DEATH.

SEE Tholuck's "*Blüthensammlung aus der Morgenländischen Mystik,*" p. 69.

I.

A PAGAN king tormented fiercely all
Who would not on his senseless idols call,
Nor worship them: and him were brought before
A mother and her child, with many more.
The child, fast bound, was flung into the flame;
Her faith the mother did in fear disclaim:
But when she cried, "O sweetest, live as I!"
He answered: "Mother dear, I do not die;
Come, mother—bliss of heaven is here my gain,
Although I seem to you in fiery pain.
This fire serves only for your eyes to cheat:
Like Jesus' breath of balm, 'tis cool and sweet.*
Come, learn what riches with our God are stored,
And how he feeds me at the angelic board.
Come, prove this fire; like water-floods it cools,
While your world's water burns like sulphur-pools.

* The Mohammedans believe that in the *breath* of Christ the healing virtue lay, by which his miraculous cures were effected.

Come—Abraham's secret, when he found alone
Sweet roses in the furnace, here is known.*
Into a world of death thou barest me—
O mother, death, not life, I owed to thee!
Fair world I deemed it once of glorious pride,
Till in this furnace I was deified;
But now I know it for a dungeon-tomb,
Since God has brought me into larger room.
Oh! now at length I live: from my pure heaven
Each cloud, that stained it once, away is driven:
Come, mother, come, and with thee many bring;
Cry, 'Here is spread the banquet of the King!'
Come, all ye faithful, come, and dare to prove
The bitter-sweet, the pain and bliss of love."

So cried the child unto that crowd of men;
All hearts with fiery longings kindled then:
Toward the pile they headlong rushing came,
And soon their souls fed sweetly on the flame.

II.

A DEWDROP, falling on the wild sea-wave,
Exclaimed in fear, "I perish in this grave!"—
But, in a shell received, that drop of dew
Unto a pearl of marvellous beauty grew;

* It is a tradition, alike Jewish and Mohammedan, that Abraham was flung into a furnace by Nimrod, for refusing to worship his false gods; whereupon the flames, instead of scorching and consuming, were turned for him into a bed of jasmine and roses.

And, happy now, the grace did magnify
Which thrust it forth, as it had feared, to die;-
Until again, "I perish quite!" it said,
Torn by rude diver from its ocean-bed:
Oh, unbelieving!—so it came to gleam,
Chief jewel in a monarch's diadem.

III.

THE seed must die, before the corn appears
Out of the ground, in blade and fruitful ears.
Low have those ears before the sickle lain,
Ere thou canst treasure up the golden grain.
The grain is crushed, before the bread is made;
And the bread broke, ere life to man conveyed.
Oh! be content to die, to be laid low,
And to be crushed, and to be broken so,
If thou upon God's table may'st be bread,
Life-giving food for souls an-hungerèd.

THE SUPPLIANT.

See *the Same*, p. 84.

All night the lonely suppliant prayed,
All night his earnest crying made;
Till, standing by his side at morn,
The Tempter said in bitter scorn:—
"Oh, peace!—what profit do you gain
From empty words and babblings vain?
'Come, Lord—oh, come!' you cry alway;
You pour your heart out night and day;
Yet still no murmur of reply—
No voice that answers, 'Here am I.'"

Then sank that stricken heart in dust,
That word had withered all its trust;
No strength retained it now to pray,
For Faith and Hope had fled away:
And ill that mourner now had fared,
Thus by the Tempter's art ensnared,
But that at length beside his bed
His sorrowing angel stood, and said:—

"Doth it repent thee of thy love,
That never now is heard above
Thy prayer, that now not any more
It knocks at heaven's gate as before?"

—"I am cast out—I find no place,
No hearing at the throne of grace:
'Come, Lord—oh, come!' I cry alway;
I pour my heart out night and day;
Yet never until now have won
The answer—'Here am I, my son.'"

—"Oh, dull of heart! enclosed doth lie,
In each 'Come, Lord,' a 'Here am I.'
Thy love, thy longing, are not thine,
Reflections of a love divine:
Thy very prayer to thee was given,
Itself a messenger from heaven.
Whom God rejects, they are not so;
Strong bands are round them in their wo;
Their hearts are bound with bands of brass,
That sigh or crying can not pass.
All treasures did the Lord impart
To Pharaoh, save a contrite heart:
All other gifts unto his foes
He freely gives, nor grudging knows;
But Love's sweet smart, and costly pain,
A treasure for his friends remain."

GHAZEL.

I.

WHAT is the good man and the wise?
Ofttimes a pearl which none doth prize:

II.

Or jewel rare, which men account
A common pebble, and despise.

III.

Set forth upon the world's bazar,
It mildly gleams, but no one buys—

IV.

Till it in anger Heaven withdraws
From the world's undiscerning eyes:

V.

And in its shell the pearl again,
And in its mine the jewel lies.

THE FALCON'S REWARD.

THIS story, at its root so similar to that of "Beth Gellert," is told in the "Calila and Dimna," and I believe is to be found in many other quarters.

I.

BENEATH the fiery cope of middle day
The youthful prince, his train left all behind,
With eager eye gazed round him every way,
If springing well he anywhere might find.

II.

His favorite falcon, from long aëry flight
Returning, and from quarry struck at last,
Told of the chase, which with its keen delight
Had thus allured him on so far and fast—

III.

Till gladly he had welcomed in his drought
The dullest pool that gathered in the rain;
But such, or fount of clearer wave, he sought
Long through that blasted, barren waste, in vain.

IV.

What pleasure when, slow stealing o'er a rock,
He spied the glittering of a little rill,
Which yet, as if his burning thirst to mock,
Did its scant treasures drop by drop distil!

V.

A golden goblet from his saddle-bow
He loosed, and from his steed alighted down,
To wait until that fountain, trickling slow,
Should in the end his golden goblet crown.

VI.

When set beside the promise of that draught,
How poor had seemed to him the costliest wine,
That with its beaded bubbles winked and laughed—
When set beside that nectar more divine!

VII.

The brimming vessel to his lips at last
He raised—when, lo! the falcon on his hand,
With beak and pinion's sudden impulse, cast
That cup's rare treasure all upon the sand.

VIII.

Long was it ere the fountain, pulsing slow,
Caused once again that chalice to run o'er;
When, thinking no like hindrance now to know,
He raised it to his parchèd lips once more:

IX.

Once more, as if to cross his purpose bent,
The watchful bird—as if on this one thing,
That drink he should not of that stream, intent—
Struck from his hand the cup with eager wing.

X.

But when this new defeat his purpose found,
Swift penalty this time the bird must pay;
Hurled down with angry force upon the ground,
Before her master's feet in death she lay:

XI.

And he, twice baffled, did meanwhile again
From that scant rill to slake his thirst prepare—
When, down the crags descending, of his train
One cried, "O monarch, for thy life forbear!

XII.

"Coiled in these waters at their fountain-head,
And causing them so feebly to distil,
A poisonous snake of hugest growth lies dead,
And doth with venom all the streamlet fill."

XIII.

Dropped from his hand the cup—one look he cast
Upon the faithful creature at his feet;
Whose dying struggles now were almost past,
For whom a better guerdon had been meet—

XIV.

Then homeward rode in silence many a mile:
  But if such thoughts did in his bosom grow,
As did in mine the painfulness beguile
  Of that his falcon's end, what man can know?

XV.

I said: "Such chalices the world fills up
  For us, and bright and without bale they seem—
A sparkling potion in a jewelled cup,
  Nor know we drawn from what infected stream.

XVI.

"Our spirit's thirst they promise to assuage,
  And we those cups unto our death had quaffed,
If Heaven did not in dearest love engage
  To dash the chalice down, and mar the draught.

XVII.

"Alas for us, if we that love are fain
  With wrath and blind impatience to repay,
Which nothing but our weakness doth restrain—
  As he repaid his faithful bird that day:

XVIII.

"If an indignant glance we lift above,
  To lose some sparkling goblet discontent,
Which, but for that keen watchfulness of love,
  Swift-circling poison through our veins had sent."

EASTERN MORALITIES.

I.

"WHO truly strives?" they asked.—Then one replied:
"The man who owns no other goal beside
The throne of God, and, till he there arrives,
Allows himself no rest, he truly strives."

II.

Honor each thing for that it once may be,
In bud the rose, in egg the chicken see;
Bright butterfly behold in ugly worm,
And trust that man enfolds an angel form.

III.

My friends exclaimed, who saw me bowed with wo:—
"Be of good cheer; the world is ebb and flow."
"To the dead fish what helps it," I replied,
"That back returns the free and flowing tide?"

IV.

A pebble, thrown into the mighty sea,
Sinks, and disturbs not its tranquillity:
No ocean, but a shallow pool, the man
Whom every little wrong disquiet can.

V.

A monk that once did at a king's board feed,
Ate less than was his wont, and was his need;
And the meal done, when he a grace should say,
Prayed more and longer than he used to pray.
O friend, if great things may in small be found,
Quite other road than heavenward thou art bound.

VI.

THE TRUE FRIEND.

He is a friend, who, treated as a foe,
Now even more friendly than before doth show;
Who to his brother still remains a shield,
Although a sword for him his brother wield;
Who of the very stones against him cast,
Builds Friendship's altar higher and more fast.

VII.

PRIDE.

With needle's point more easily you will
Uproot and quite unfasten a huge hill,
Than from the bosom you will dig up pride;
And the ant's footfall sooner is descried,
On black earth moving, in the darkest night,
Than are pride's secret movements brought to light.

VIII.

The business of the world is child's play mere;
Too many, ah! the children playing here:
Their pleasure and their wo, their loss and gain,
Alike mean nothing, and alike are vain—

As children's, who, to pass the time away,
Build up their booths, and buy and sell in play;
But homeward hungering must at eve repair,
And standing leave their booths with all their ware:
So the world's children, when *their* night is come,
With empty satchels turn them sadly home.

IX.

Sage, that wouldst maker of thine own God be,
When made, alas! what will he profit thee?
Most like art thou to children that astride
On reeds or wooden horses proudly ride;
And as they trail them on the ground, they cry,
"This is the lightning, and its Lord am I!"
Yet, while they deem their horses them upbear,
Themselves the bearers of their horses are;
And when they grow aweary of their course,
They find no strength in them, no help, no force.
How otherwise they fare, how fresh, how strong,
Not of themselves, but borne of God along!
How jubilant to him they lift their head,
Till the ninth heaven shakes underneath their tread!

X.

SCIENCE AND LOVE.

Who that might watch the moon in heaven, would look
At its weak image in the water-brook?
Who were content, that might in presence stand
Of one beloved, with letters from his hand?

When thou hast learned the name, hast thou the thing?
What life to thee will definitions bring?
Will the four letters, R, O, S, and E,
The rose's hues and fragrance bring to thee?
Feed not on husks, but these strip off and feed
On the rich kernel, which is food indeed.
Say, who of choice would wash in arid sand,
While limpid streams were bubbling close at hand?
Bare Science is dry sand: thy spirit's wings
Bathe thou in Love's delicious water-springs.
Be thou the bee, which ever to its cell
Not wax alone, but honey brings as well:
Good is the wax for light, but better still
What will thy hive with storèd sweetness fill.

XI.

THE GIFT IN THE TEMPLE.

His splendid pilgrimage to Mecca done,
Within the temple great Almansur's son
Showered with a bounty prodigal and proud
Enormous gifts among the struggling crowd;
And every day those gifts he multiplied,
Vexed every day and humbled in his pride,
That one who seemed the poorest pilgrim there,
Remained aloof with calm, abstracted air
Indifferent, and contended not nor pressed,
To share his scattered largess with the rest.

Until at last, when he had shed in vain
Gold, jewels, pearls, he could no more refrain,
But cried to him, "And dost thou naught desire,
And wilt thou nothing at my hands require?"
Who answered, standing where before he stood:—
"Great shame it were for me, if any good,
While thus within the house of God I stand,
I asked or looked for, saving at his hand."

XII.

See Von Hammer's "*Geschichte der schönen Redekünste Persiens,*" p. 389.

Man, the caged bird that owned a higher nest,
Is here awhile detained, reluctant guest;
Plumage and beak he shatters in his rage,
And with his prison doth vain war engage;
For him the falcon watches, and his snare
The bloody fowler doth for him prepare.
Exiled from home, he here doth sadly sing,
In spring lacks autumn, and in autumn spring.
Far from his nest, he shivers on a wall,
Where blows on him of rude misfortune fall—
His head with weight of misery sore bowed down,
His pinion clogged with dust, his courage gone.
Then from his nest in heaven is heard a cry,
And straight he spreads his wings divine on high:
Lift him, O Lord, unto the lotus-tree,
No meaner pitch may with his birth agree;

Grant him a pinion of such lofty flight,
That he may on the lotus-tree alight:
In thy bright palaces his nest prepare;
Oh, happy, happy bird that nesteth there!

XIII.

MAN'S TWOFOLD NATURE.

A HEN, though such tame creatures mostly are,
Yet once received a water-bird in care:
Its mother-instinct drew the fledgling still
To the wide ocean-floods, to roam at will;
Its timid nurse, upon the other hand,
Sought evermore to lead it back to land.
O man! thy mother, Heaven, thy nurse is Earth,
And thou of both wert nurtured from thy birth:
From thy true mother comes thine impulse free
To launch forth boldly upon being's sea;
While aye thy nurse fears for thee, and would fain
Thee to a narrow slip of dry restrain.
Up, and remember Adam's kingly worth,
How angels danced before him at his birth—
How unto him they rendered homage all,
And served him at the glorious festival,
The bridal of two worlds, that kissed and met
The morn when he in paradise was set.
Up, man! for what if thou with beasts hast part,
Since in the body framed of dust thou art?

Yet know thyself upon the other side
Higher than angels, and to God allied.
But ah! I sound this high alarum in vain,
Sunk on thy bosom doth thy head remain:
In lists of love, while noblest bosoms bleed,
That flies not vex thee, this is all thy heed.
Up! be a man at last; with Abraham go
From house and kindred forth, thy God to know:
Fair shine the sun, and moon, and host of heaven—
To eye of sense no fairer sight is given;
Yet cry with him: "These rise to set again;
I worship Him, a light that will not wane."
Into the wilderness with Moses hie,
And hear that mighty word, "The Lord am I!"
Then hast thou won the place that is thine own,
A sitter on the threshold of God's throne.

GENOVEVA

AND OTHER POEMS.

GENOVEVA.

In times such as these, when it is more than ever a duty to put no offence in the way of any, I may as well mention that, in the versifying of this tale, I have no more than sought accurately to follow the old legend: in doing which I have not considered that the abuse of the forms of medieval piety, which is committed when they are sought to be thrust upon us afresh, is any reason for omitting them in my version of the legend; seeing that, with whatever error mixed up, they were yet the genuine shapes under which earnest godliness manifested itself in those ages to which this story belongs.

I.

As the finest crystal still
Bides the most exposed to ill—
As the finest crystal, ever
Brittlest, may the soonest shiver—
So in this world fares no less
With some rarer happiness:
Such a happiness was thine,
Siegfried, count and palatine,
When thou leddest home thy bride,
When thou watchedst her in pride,
As all eyes did on her wait,
Moving in her queenly state—
Genoveva, fairest flower
Blooming in Brabantine bower
Once, and now transferred to dwell
On the banks of fair Moselle.

'Twas in sooth a golden time,
And the world was in its prime
For them two;—the sun stood high
Of their rare felicity—
Standing right above their head,
Did no way a shadow shed.
  But this might not always last;
Happy months too soon have past:
Charles has called from east and west
All who own his high behest;
Charles has bid from far and near
All his liegemen to appear.
For must now at length be met,
Now must have its boundaries set
That wild tide of Moslem war,
Which has rolled so fierce and far—
Issuing from Arabian sands,
Overflowing mightiest lands,
Till it reached to western Spain,
And has burst o'er Aquitaine,
And is panting to advance
To the very heart of France.
At the gate are trumpets sounding,
And impatient chargers bounding,
And a numerous, proud array
Only for their chieftain stay;
And he comes—in lady's bowers
'Tis no time to waste the hours:

Who this precious time would choose
In ignoble ease to lose,
While by others fields are fought,
Glorious deeds by others wrought,
While by other hearts and hands
France is freed from miscreant bands?
Nor would she her lord detain,
Though her arms are like a chain,
That will scarce relax again;
Though when now the latest note
Of the trump in air doth float,
By her maidens she is found
Without motion on the ground,
In a deep and heavy swoon;
But from thence reviving soon,
Doth her widowed state beguile,
Cheers the sad and lonely while,
Not with shows or pageantries,
Not with pomps or revelries,
But with prayer and vigil long,
With the church's solemn song,
Stirring so the malice fell
And the deepest hate of hell.

II.

Well thou farest, gallant count,
Foremost in the battle brunt,

Foremost on that famous field,
When to Heaven two faiths appealed,
When seven times uprose the sun
And the battle was not done,
And six times went down the day
On an undecided fray:
Well thou speedest; to thy king
No mean help thy hand did bring
On that last day, when he smote
Many a Moslem's mailèd coat—
When his ponderous blows so well
Like on ringing anvil fell,
That to him henceforth the name
Of "The Hammer" justly came.
Well thou farest—better far
Than that sadly-gleaming star,
Thou didst leave to shine alone
In thy sphere, when thou art gone—
Better than that lonely dove
Fond of heart, and true of love,
Who within her widowed bowers
Counts the tardy-pacing hours.
What a mist of hell obscure
Gathers round thy planet pure!
What a serpent coils and clings
Round thy fair dove's silver wings!
What of hellish wiles are met
Round about her, to beset

First the honor, then the life
Of that ever-faithful wife!
  Ill didst thou, O count, provide,
Setting at thy lady's side,
For thy holy home to guard,
And to keep due watch and ward,
One who there such watch doth keep
As the wolf on silly sheep:
Such a guard the kite would prove
To the weakness of the dove.
Evil man! who when there fell
On his bosom sparks of hell,
Did not, as alone was meet,
Stamp them underneath his feet,
With an indignation keen
That such thoughts should once have been;
But those sparks of foul desire
Left to kindle to a fire—
Fed and fanned them, till they grew
Such a mighty flame unto,
As will not be quenched, before
One it has consumed, or more.
—He has dared to tell his tale;
She, with fear and anger pale,
Twice must hear, but when the third
Time this suit of shame she heard,
Then exclaimed: "Thy lord shall know
Whom he has intrusted so:

Evil meed wilt thou have earned,
When thy lord has back returned;
Twice forgiven—but twice in vain—
Hence! nor see my face again."
Forth the caitiff went, and told
To his mother, weird and old,
Full of evil plots and wiles,
Full of treacheries and guiles,
All his danger and his fear:—
—"Help me, or my death is near;
Give me counsel, or I die:
One must perish—she or I!"

III.

Innocence is fearless still—
Means not and suspects not ill.
Of the band that waited near
Genoveva, one was dear—
For his piety beloved,
And with many signs approved
Of her grace: his tender age
Did he unto God engage,
Who, before her kneeling, read
From an open scroll outspread,
Where were written records high
Of the Christian chivalry;
Of young Agnes, tender flower,
Gathered in her childhood's hour;

And of patient Laurence, spread
Calmly on his fiery bed;
Of Eulalia, whose fair corse,
Flung abroad without remorse,
From a higher care must know
Its pure winding-sheet of snow;
And of them that bore so well
All the spite of earth and hell,
Whose dear ashes forth were thrown
To make rich her neighboring Rhone;
And of many more beside,
In extremest tortures tried;
Names that never shall grow old,
Hearts to servile fear unsold,
Holy virgins, martyrs bold,
Lilies those of dazzling white,
Roses these with red hues dight,
In the garden of the Lord;—
With a pensive ear she heard,
With a spirit inly wrought,
Marvelling in secret thought,
How the holiest and most pure
Most were given to endure;
How it still was theirs to drain
Deepest cups of mortal pain.

But these musings must have end,
Must reveal what they portend.

Hark! a noise is heard without,
Then a rude, inrushing rout,
Led of him who should no more
Dare to stand her face before.
Up she started in surprise;
All the coming on her eyes
Flashing in a moment rose—
The long order of her woes,
The foul tale, the hateful lie,
And the deep-laid villany.
Knew she now what cup of pain
Unto her was given to drain;
Her as well that cup had found,
Had unto her lips come round.
"Ha!" that faithless guardian cried,
When the wondering twain he spied,
"It was this, even this I thought,
And my fears to proof are brought.
Have we not endured this wrong
Done against our lord too long?
Hence! away with both—away!
Hence! nor heed them, what they say;
Mine the charge, that without stain
My lord's honor should remain:
If this may not be, at least
Shall the rank offence have ceased.
Bear him to his death—her doom
She shall wait in dungeon-gloom!"

IV.

Such a mist of hell obscure
Gathers round that planet pure,
Such a serpent coils and clings
Round that fair dove's silver wings,
Such of hellish wiles are met,
And such treacheries to beset
First the honor, then the life,
Of that ever-faithful wife;
While the count do spaces wide,
Streams and mountains, still divide
From his periled lady's side.
For, with slow and sullen pace,
Turning oftentimes the face,
Afric's swarthy hosts retreat
From the field of their defeat;—
As with many a pause of pride
Ebbeth a reluctant tide,
Slowly on its refluent track
Is with many a pause drawn back,
Oft with new-awakened roar
Winneth ground again, before
It has quite left bare the shore—
As a lion from his prey
By the hunters scared away,
Who, though now no more remaining,
Yet the show of flight disdaining,

Often turns, and makes his stand,
Glares on the pursuing band,
Till the shepherds back recoil,
Winning no unbloody spoil.
And the gallant count of Trêves,
Though by night and day he weaves
Visions of his happy home—
Though full oft his fancies roam
From the camp's tumultuous noise,
From the battle's heady joys,
To the banks of fair Moselle,
Where for him all good things dwell—
Though he yearns for quick release
Unto scenes of holy peace—
Yet will faithfully abide
By his noble captain's side,
Till into the western seas,
Or beyond the Pyrenees,
Is the latest foeman urged,
And the land is throughly purged.
Joy to him! for tidings come,
Letters from his distant home.
Joy it is not—he doth stand,
Those crushed letters in his hand,
And men speak, but meaning none
From their speech his ear has won;
O'er the world doth blackness pass,
Black the sunlight on the grass,

Black the sun itself—on all
Blackness falls, a murky pall.
The firm heavens are round him wheeling,
The fixed earth beneath him reeling;
Oh, the cunning web of hell!
Oh, the treachery woven too well!
—"Genoveva! oh, no, no—
Yet it is, it must be so.
Oh, 'twas well and bravely done;
Thou thy master's praise hast won,
Who didst boldly use thy power,
And didst cast her in that hour
To a dungeon out of sight.
Would that she had died outright—
Died with him, and shared his fate,
In this sin her guilty mate!
Better so—but let her die
With the child of infamy—
Child of infamy and scorn
That was in the dungeon born!"
With this message he in part
The wild tumult of his heart
Has assuaged—some ease has won:
—Yet, oh think, was this well done,
Was it with thine own heart well,
When in it such thoughts could dwell?
If thy spirit had drawn breath
In the worlds of loftiest faith,

Couldst thou have been so deceived?—
Wouldst thou not have then believed
Everything on earth a lie,
Ere thy lady's purity?

V.

Lo! a woman strangely fair,
With her wildly-streaming hair,
All alone, companionless,
In a savage wilderness:—
Now she kneels with arms stretched out,
Now she strangely roams about;
Underneath a thorn-tree's shade
Wailing infant she has laid,
Like another Hagar flying,
That she may not see him dying.
—"From that cry—that cry of pain—
Still I flee, but still in vain:
Whither, whither shall I fly?
All the fountains are drawn dry
Of my bosom utterly:
With its milk my child at first,
Till that wholly failed, I nursed;
Then the blood away it drew,
And now that has failed me too.
Oh! what helps it that the twain,
Who were charged to end my pain,

Have withheld the murderous knife
From my own and infant's life,
(While I promised never more
To appear men's eyes before,)
If they leave us here to die
With a longer agony?
—O my husband! other thought
Was it that within me wrought,
Then, when from my height of place
Fell I to that strange disgrace,
And that scorn extreme must prove:
In thy faith and in thy love
Found I still a refuge strong
From that uttermost of wrong.
'Twas enough the hours were flowing,
'Twas enough the days were going,
That would bring thee to my side,
All that dark mist scattering wide.
God and Savior! and thine ear
Doth it not our crying hear?
God and Savior! is thine eye
Closèd on our misery?
Are the springs of love divine
Dry as are these breasts of mine?
When my little one has died,
What have I on earth beside?"
  Round she gazed, if anywhere
Dawned a glimpse of comfort there:

Not a human step was near,
Not a human voice to cheer,
And no angel-comforter
In her anguish spake to her.
Oh, how darkly desolate,
Oh, how full of scorn and hate
At that moment seemed all Nature—
Every mute and senseless creature;
All upon her misery
Gazing with unpitying eye!
Danced the light leaves in the air,
As deriding her despair;
Echoes came in idle mocks,
Tossed from the unfeeling rocks;
Merrily the stream tripped on,
Gloriously the gay sun shone,
Stretched the breadth of azure sky
Like a banner upon high:
But no pity anywhere
Might she find, no love, no care:
Dark the earth, forlorn of love,
But, oh! darker heaven above—
God's own heaven seemed darker yet.
But this deadliest thought is met:
She hath prayed, and doth repel
This the deadliest shaft of hell;
She hath prayed, and not in vain;
Faith returns to her again;

And when now the feeble crying,
The faint moanings of the dying,
Faint and fainter, wholly cease,
God she thanks that all is peace;
That her infant findeth rest
On a loving Savior's breast.
She with all is reconciled;
Once will look upon her child,
Then its little body lay
In the deepest grave she may.

Near she draws, and yet more near,
Not a stirring may she hear:
But what other sight her eyes
Welcomed with a glad surprise!
Near the boy a gentle doe
Knelt, as white as mountain-snow,
And with eager lips the child
From that loving creature mild
Drew the sweetest nourishment,
Which, for its own offspring sent,
Now to him it freely lent.
When the mother from above
Bent on him her looks of love,
He at length began to stir—
Did his little hands to her
Stretch, and turn in gladsome wise
On her face his laughing eyes:

What sweet tears from hers were shed!
What new faith in her was bred!
Here will she abide, until
Life shall finish, and life's ill,
Housing in a hollow cave—
Shelter, when the wild winds rave;
Here, where God this grace did send,
She will calmly wait the end.

VI.

Blindly, blindly, in the dark
Welters now his spirit's bark,
Who has blotted from his heaven
All the lights to guide him given—
So that now there doth endure
Unto him no good, no pure,
And no virtue seemeth sure;
While the fairest form wherein
Goodness did a body win,
Leprous all have showed with sin;
While the star which he well-nigh
Worshipped, where it shone on high,
Suddenly has left its height,
Treacherous meteor of the night.
Round his path is darkness spread;
But what thicker night is shed

Then, when he is undeceived,
And has all the web unweaved
Of that hateful treachery,
Of that foul and hideous lie;
When the traitor owns his guilt,
And his blood is justly spilt—
And a murderer *thou* dost stand,
With her blood upon thy hand!
Oh! what profits now the force
Of thy measureless remorse?
What thy soul's strong agonies?
What thy tears of blood, thy cries
Underneath the midnight skies?
What a thousand anguished years,
An eternity of tears?
All were profitless to rue
What a single hour could do.
Wilt thou call her from the tomb?
Wilt thou bid her from the gloom
Of that forest, where she lies
Hidden deep from human eyes?

Faithful mother! truest wife!
Hardly she sustains her life
In that wasteful wilderness:
Oh, unparalleled distress!
Who, that paints it to his thought,
Would not unto tears be brought?

She, a child of Flanders' earl,
Lacking what the meanest churl,
Poorest beggar that did wait
At her sire's or husband's gate,
Had not lacked—of which bereft,
She had not the meanest left.
Changed she has her palace-dome
For a cave of damp and gloom;
Maidens wait not her about,
But wild beasts go in and out;
And no other music more
Knows she than their sullen roar;
For a soft and downy bed,
Sticks are underneath her spread;
She has left her dainty food
For the harsh roots of the wood;
Pearls she has not—in their place
Tears are on her wo-worn face;
Only jewels now she knew
Were the drops of chilly dew,
Hanging on the pointed thorn:
This is now her state forlorn.

While the days are summer-long,
Then her pains are not so strong;
While the days are summer-warm,
She may shield her child from harm.
Oh! but when the leaves now sere
Told of pitiless winter near,

How she shuddered then to know
What she soon must undergo!
Ill with her it then did fare,
Then her pains were hard to bear.
She must melt within her mouth
Ice, when she would slake her drouth;
When her hunger would allay,
Must the hard snow scrape away,
Till the roots at length she found,
Buried deep in frozen ground.
How amid the long nights dark,
When the cold was stiff and stark,
When the icy north-wind blew,
Keen sword, piercing through and through,
Searching, as it fiercely drave,
Every corner of the cave—
Oh, how then that mother prest
Her poor shiverer to her breast!
Though no moisture that could give—
Warmth not any there did live;
And, herself forgetting quite,
Wailed for that poor, shuddering wight;
Who, beholding her to weep,
And that long, low wail to keep,
Wailed and wept himself as well,
Though his grief he could not tell.
  Yet, amid her keenest ill,
She in God found comfort still;

And when day by day the doe
Through the ice and through the snow
Came—a constant visitant,
To that poor child ministrant—
Blest assurance, token clear
Of his grace, she welcomed here:—
It may be, now thanked him more
Than she ever thanked before;
Could his wondrous guidance praise,
That had from the world's vain ways,
From its flatteries and its wiles,
From its heart-deluding smiles,
Her delivered, and had brought,
By rough paths she had not sought—
But which now she could discern,
And their gracious meaning learn—
To this shelter safe, though stern.

VII.

Mourned this painful hermitess
Of the lonely wilderness—
Lowly kneeling, mourned one day,
Did with eyes uplifted pray,
In a trance-like agony
Sunken, when she seemed to see,
From that bright, superior coast,
One of its angelic host

Stooping toward her;—awful fear
In his visage did appear,
And his front was bent before
That which in his hand he bore:
Only hands of angels ought
Lovely as that cross had wrought,
With the image there suspended,
In which Love and Death contended;
And this cross he reached to her—
This angelic comforter;
And her agony beguiled
With these soothing words and mild:—
"Genoveva, take thou this;
Take it for the boon it is,
Choicest blessing, costliest boon,
That God's treasure-house doth own,
Gift he keepeth for his friends,
And to thee at this time sends.
Hither be thy glances sent,
When thy soul with pangs is rent;
Set on this thine eyes and heart,
When impatient movements start;
This shall as a shield repel
All the fiery darts of hell;
This shall prove a golden key,
Heaven unlocking unto thee."

Was it vision? was it truth?
Dream, or very waking sooth?

Did a heavenly messenger,
Did an angel, talk with her?
She hath started from her trance,
Round she flings a timorous glance;
There doth no one now appear
By her side, far off or near:
Yet in rocky niche upright,
Plain before her waking sight,
Lo! a crucifix—it stands
Beauteous, as if angel-hands
Had that ivory work divine
Wrought into salvation's sign,
This in summer she alway
Did adorn with flowery may—
Ever decked it as she could,
With the wild-flowers of the wood;
Nor in barest winter left
Of all ornament bereft,
But with mosses would entwine,
Or with dark, unfading pine.
Here her solace found she still
In extremities of ill,
In her Savior's five wounds laid
All her griefs, her anguish stayed:
Here, when once she did complain,
Uttering words of hasty pain—
"Jesu, Savior, what is this?
What have I so much amiss

Wrought, how sinnèd against thee
More than all, that I should be
For a vile adulteress
Driven into this wilderness,
To this anguish and this shame?"
Seemed it then that accents came
From that cross, and named her name:—
"Genoveva, is it well
At my chastening to rebel?
Are thy sufferings more than mine?
Or had I more guilt than thine?
Yet was I put forth from heaven;
By my Father I was given
To my cross and mortal wo:
Look on me, and, looking, so
Learn to bear thy present ill,
And what thou must suffer still."
This her Savior's mild rebuke
To her heart with shame she took,
And no word of discontent,
Whatsoever griefs he sent,
Did she ever speak again,
But her passion and her pain
Did with meekest heart sustain—
Yea, did welcome and approve
For the gifts of highest love.
 Then she found how wildest creatures—
How the wild-wood's savage natures

At Heaven's bidding could be made
Ministers to yield her aid:
Came the wolf, yet not to harm,
But a shaggy sheepskin warm
In his teeth one day he bore;
This he cast the child before,
In its woolly folds henceforth
Shielded from the bitterest north;
And the beasts to him grew tame,
Round him without fear they came—
Came the gentle creatures near,
Without fierceness, without fear;
As he wandered through the wood,
With their speaking gestures showed
What were harmful herbs and good—
With the boy made pastime; he
Of the wilderness was free—
Rode upon the wolf, and played
With the swift hair on the glade;
Round his head the birds would flit,
On his hand the birds alit;
And the mother and the child
Of their misery oft beguiled
With melodious descants wild.
And as he to more years grew,
Lacked she not some comfort new;
Sweetest words with him she changed,
Whence her heart was oft estranged

Of the grief which on it lay—
Taught him in what words to pray,
How he should "Our Father" say,
And his little hands above
Lift unto a God of love,
Who was watching for them still,
Who, in midst of all their ill,
For the desolate had cared:—
Thus with them long while it fared.

VIII.

But the count, whom prosperous hours
Back to his ancestral towers
Bring, and to his widowed bowers,
How shall he, this lone man, bear
The approach and entrance there?
Lonely man! though at his side
Troops of friends and vassals ride;
Lonely man! though at his gate
Him ten thousand welcomes wait;
Heart unwelcomed home, although
Thousand voices skyward go;
Thousand voices fill the air,
But the one is lacking there!
How shall he endure to pace
Those long-echoing halls, and trace
Each remembered happy place,

Haunted each with its own ghost
Of some ancient splendor lost,
Each with its own vision bright
Of some forfeited delight
Rising clear upon his sight?
How beside a cold hearth stand,
Quenched by his own reckless hand?
He has borne it, man forlorn!
Borne—for all things may be borne;
And he lives, nor freedom asks
From life's ordinary tasks,
Him though oft the crowded hall,
And the thronging festival,
With that dreariest sense oppress
Of a peopled wilderness;
Though the crowds that to and fro
On their busy errands go,
Ofttimes seem with all their tasks
But so many gibbering masks;
Though he oft must contemplate
The strange mockeries of Fate,
Which with hand profuse had shed
Gifts so many on his head—
Which had lent him splendor, fame,
And a glory round his name—
Honor, due to him whose hand
Helped to free his native land;

Yet withdrew the single thing
Which to all a worth would bring.—

And the years give no relief,
Mellowing an austerer grief;
But a melancholy dim,
Dark and darker, fell on him.
Round him, when his state they knew,
Friends and faithful kinsmen drew,
With consoling words and speech,
Which his heart's wound can not reach:
Yet he strives not, when the morn
They will greet with hawk and horn;
Still he yields a sad consent,
Is with everything content,
Feast, or chase, or tournament.
"Brother," so to him one day
Did his faithful kinsman say—
"Oft a milk-white hind is seen
On that belt of tender green,
Skirting the dark forest vast
We so many times have past:
Seen it flieth, but with flight
As it would pursuit invite;
Though remaining unpursued
In that deep and haunted wood
To this hour.—With hound and horn
We will rouse to-morrow morn:

And methinks we shall not there
Fail to find some quarry rare,
That or other, which shall greet
Friends that here to-morrow meet."

IX.

It is day: with hound and horn
They have roused that morrow morn—
Have the milk-white creature found
On that edge of grassy ground,
And with eager steps pursued
Far into the gloomy wood;
Till the hunters, one by one,
By the length of way foredone,
Rein their steeds—but onward still,
Thorough brake and over hill,
Down steep glen, through foaming river,
Doth Count Siegfried follow ever.
Wild and wilder grows the scene;
Seems it step of man hath been
Never in this savage place:
He too now foregoes the chase,
For he sees another sight
Which hath shook him with the might,
Brave albeit, of strange affright.

—"Who art thou, by none befriended,
Only of that hind attended,
Which has fled with steps so fleet
To the refuge of thy feet—
Housing in the desert's heart,
From all Christian souls apart?
Who art thou? come forth and tell
If a sprite of heaven or hell?"
—"Shall I in thy sight appear,
Cast me in thy mantle here,
Else I can not without blame
Stand before thee."—Forth she came,
Wrapped in it; there stood also
By her side the fearless doe.
—"Here of free choice dwell I not,
But have still my God besought
He would guide of his good grace
Human steps to this drear place.
He has heard those prayers of mine,
And has guided even thine.
What of me thou fain wouldst know,
I too willingly will show:
I, this wretched and forlorn
Woman, in Brabant was born;
No ignoble stock was mine,
For I came of princely line;
But must find in worst distress
Shelter in this wilderness,

When my husband erringly
Of my truth misdeemed, and me
With my infant would have then
Slain by hands of evil men."
  Then exceeding tremblings came
Over all Count Siegfried's frame.
On her face a fixed regard
Turned he—that was all so marred,
He could read no history there—
"But thy name and his declare!"
—"If my own self I have not,
As the world has me, forgot,
I am Genoveva hight."
From his steed he fell outright
On the moment when she came
To the syllabling that name;
Down upon his face he fell,
As by stroke invisible
Earthward smitten—there lay long,
And his sobs were thick and strong,
Choking utterance—till his head
He a little raising, said:—
"Genoveva, can it be
That I now should look on thee,
Thee, my own, my murdered wife—
Genevieve, my love, my life?
Oh, how wan, how worn, how weak!
Oh, that eye! that sunken cheek!

Oh, the utter misery
That my guilt has brought on thee!
Canst thou, Genevieve, forgive?
Wilt thou bid this wretch to live?
Low before thy feet I lie;
Thousand deaths if I should die,
And in each a thousand years—
Drain my heart's blood out in tears,
All were nothing to my sin!
Then free pardon let me win:
Pardon for His sake I crave,
Who upon his cross forgave."
—"O my husband, all is past!
God is good, and he at last
Of his grace has brought this day.
If thou wishest, I will say
That I pardon—rise, oh rise!
With these sobs and agonies
Thou wilt kill my heart outright.
See, too, who appears in sight!—
O my sweet child, come—you may
Fling those herbs and roots away.
Fear not, sweetest, you will find
That the man is good and kind."
—"Cause too just he has to fear;
Oh, to think ye two were here
All this while, and I so near!

Thou, and he whom I am bold
To a father's heart to fold."
  But enough: what words can tell
Of a joy unspeakable—
Of the trancèd, long embrace,
(In his bosom hid her face,)
With its gush of mingling tears,
Worth a thousand torturing years?
  Others have arrived, to share
In the holy gladness there;
Through the forest tidings fly,
And all draw in wonder nigh.
Near her timidly they draw,
And they kiss her feet in awe,
While to them she doth appear
Creature of another sphere.
Faith they scarcely will afford
To the assurance of their lord,
'Tis their mistress lost so long,
Overliving all her wrong.
Now a litter is in haste
Of green branches interlaced,
And on it their lady borne,
By her grief and joy outworn.
Yet or ever from that spot,
From that stern and rugged grot
Genoveva turned away,
Lowly kneeling will she pay

Thankful vows from grateful heart,
Ere she from that cave depart,
For the mercy and the grace
Which had found her in that place;
Kissed with tears the holy rood,
Where in rocky niche it stood:
—"Fare thee well! I leave thee here,
For so many memories dear;
Thou a shield that didst repel
All the fiery darts of hell;
Thou that wast a golden key,
Heaven unlocking unto me.
With these tears once more I say
Fare thee well—I go away;
But what here has been my gain,
May it with me still remain!"

To the castle now doth hie
A rejoicing company,
While from village and from town
Others stream to meet them soon,
As in triumph one doth bear
High in arms the new-found heir:
Round his head the glad birds flit,
Singing on his hand they sit—
Glad farewells they seem to sing,
His new fortunes welcoming.
Nor doth not the fearless doe
In the glad procession go;

Has its own peculiar dower
In the glory of this hour:
Round it shouting children press,
Smooth its sides with fond caress,
Kiss its face, and slender neck
With their flowery garlands deck,
While all praise the gentle hind,
And its ministrations kind.

X.

Joy is in Count Siegfried's bowers,
Joy upon those ancient towers,
Festal gladness in the room
Of that weight of brooding gloom;
Nor doth she, whose presence bright
Chased the darkness of that night,
Bringing back return of light,
In this joy refuse her share:
Yet another, higher care
Fills her heart—how best to keep
Those heights, difficult and steep,
Which her spirit did attain
In its years of desert pain—
Him her pattern still to own,
Wearer of the thorny crown.
To the count, as more he knows,
Ever loftier wonder grows

At her saintly virtues high—
Ay, a sadder certainty,
That he will not long retain
His new-won and glorious gain.
She doth meekly undertake
All life's tasks for his dear sake;
Yet she evermore doth seem
Like one moving in a dream,
Or as one called back from death,
Strangely drawing vital breath;
All so wondrous doth the stir
Of our life appear to her;
All so little to her mind
Doth she now its pageants find.
And not many months have been,
Ere of every eye 'tis seen
That the hour is nearly come
When the weary one will home—
Ere too plain the work appears
Of those cruel, wasting years.
Every day her pale, pale face
Wears a more unearthly grace:
Angel-wings are o'er her head,
Angel-feet about her bed:
She doth catch in trances high
Heaven's transcending melody;
Enters by heaven's golden doors,
Treads upon its sapphire floors,

And clear voices do not cease
Warning her of near release—
Sounds she may interpret well,
Wherefore sent, and what they tell;
Yet to him will not impart,
That she may not rend his heart:
For what anguish had they brought
To his soul, who well had thought
To atone that mighty wrong
By a life of service long—
By long years of service true,
And devotion ever new—
But must now seem torn and scattered,
By this stroke for ever shattered,
That fond vision, by whose art
He had many times in part
Spoken peace unto his heart!

XI.

Gently speak and lightly tread—
'Tis the chamber of the dead!
Now thine earthly course is run,
Now thy weary day is done;
Genoveva, sainted one!
Happy flight thy sprite has taken,
From its plumes earth's last dust shaken:

On the earth is passionate weeping,
Round thy bier lone vigils keeping—
In the heaven triumphant songs,
Welcome of angelic throngs,
As thou enterest on that day
Which no tears nor fears allay,
No regrets nor pangs affray,
Hemmed not in by yesterday,
By to-morrow hemmed not in.
Weep not for her—she doth win
What we long for; now is she
That which all desire to be.
Bear her forth with solemn cheer,
Bear her forth on open bier,
That the wonder which hath been
May of every eye be seen.
Wonderful! that pale, worn brow
Death hath scarcely sealed, and now
All the beauty that she wore
In the youthful years before,
All the freshness and the grace,
And the bloom upon her face,
Ere that seven-yeared distress
In the painful wilderness—
Ere that wasting sickness came,
Undermining quite her frame,
All come back—the light, the hue,
Tinge her cheek and lip anew:

Far from her, oh! far away,
All that is so quick to say—
'Man returneth to his clay:'
All that to our creeping fear
Whispers of corruption near
Seems it as she would illume
With her radiance and her bloom
The dark spaces of the tomb.

XII.

Once again thou art alone,
From that other sorrow thrown
All too quickly upon this:
Oh, few days of fleeting bliss!
Where shall they who fain would speak
Comfort now, the mourner seek?
'Mid his old ancestral towers,
His twice-desolated bowers?
On the battle-fields of Spain,
Where the hardy Goths maintain
Their Asturian mountains well,
Thrusting back the infidel?
Rather in the deep recess
Of a pathless wilderness,
Out of knowledge, out of sight,
Seek a lonely eremite.

Him has good Hidulphus blest,
Praised his purpose, and his quest
(Even before this life shall close)
Of a place of sure repose.
So a church in that wild wood
Rises, where that cross had stood:
Underneath the altar high
Genoveva's relics lie;
And that cross, of angel-hands
Wrought, above the altar stands.
He, within a rugged grot,
In the very self-same spot
Where she saw those cruel years,
Where she wept those many tears,
Dwells, where Genoveva dwelt—
Kneels, where Genoveva knelt;
From the self-same spring doth take
Water for his thirst to slake;
Often knows no other food
Than the wild roots of the wood;
Well content to undergo
Some small portion of the wo
Which so long he made her know.
There he waits for his release,
There in God finds perfect peace—
Till the long years end at last,
And he too at length has past

From the sorrow and the fears
From the anguish and the tears,
From the desolate distress,
Of this world's great loneliness—
From its withering and its blight,
From the shadow of its night,
Into God's pure sunshine bright.

ORPHEUS AND THE SIRENS.

"ORPHEUS laudes Deorum cantans et reboans, Sirenum voces confudit et summovit: meditationes enim rerum divinarum voluptates sensûs non tantum potestate, sed etiam suavitate superant." —*Lord Bacon's "Sapientia Veterum."*

I.

HIGH on the poop, with many a godlike peer,
With heroes and with kings, the flower of Greece,
That gathered at his word, from far and near,
To snatch the guarded fleece—

II.

Great Jason stood: nor ever from the soil
The anchor's brazen tooth unfastenèd,
Till, auspicating so his glorious toil,
From golden cup he shed

III.

Libations to the gods—to highest Jove,
To Waves and prospering Winds, to Night and Day,
To all by whom befriended they might prove
A favorable way.

IV.

With him the twins — one mortal, one divine —
Of Leda and the Strength of Hercules;
And Tiphys, steersman through the perilous brine,
And many more with these:

V.

Great father, Peleus, of a greater son,
And Atalanta, martial queen, was here;
And that supreme Athenian, nobler none,
And Idmon, holy seer.

VI.

Nor Orpheus pass unnamed, though from the rest
Apart, he leaned upon that lyre divine,
Which once in heaven his glory should attest,
Set there, a sacred sign:

VII.

But when auspicious thunders pealed on high,
Unto its chords and to his chant sublime
The joyful heroes, toiling manfully,
With measured strokes kept time.

VIII.

Then when that keel divided first the waves,
Them Chiron cheered from Pelion's piny crown,
And wondering sea-nymphs rose from ocean-caves,
And all the gods looked down.

IX.

The bark divine, itself instinct with life,
Went forth, and baffled ocean's rudest shocks—
Escaping, though with pain and arduous strife,
The huge encountering rocks:

X.

And force and fraud o'ercome, and peril past,
Its hard-won trophy raised in open view,
Through prosperous floods was bringing home at last
Its high, heroic crew:

XI.

Till now they cried (Ææa left behind,
And the dead waters of the Cronian main)—
"No peril more upon our path we find,
Safe haven soon we gain!"

XII.

When, as they spake, sweet sounds upon the breeze
Came to them, melodies till now unknown,
And, blended into one delight with these,
Sweet odors sweetly blown—

XIII.

Sweet odors wafted from the flowery isle,
Sweet music breathèd by the Sirens three,
Who there lie wait, all passers to beguile,
Fair monsters of the sea!

XIV.

Fair monsters foul, that with their magic song
  And beauty to the shipman wandering
Worse peril than disastrous whirlpools strong,
  Or fierce sea-robbers bring.

XV.

Sometimes upon the diamond rocks they leant,
  Sometimes they sate upon the flowery lea
That sloped towàrd the wave, and ever sent
  Shrill music o'er the sea.

XVI.

One piped, one sang, one swept the golden lyre;
  And thus to forge and fling a threefold chain
Of linkèd harmony the three conspire,
  O'er land and hoary main.

XVII.

The Winds, suspended by the charmèd song,
  Shed treacherous calm about that fatal isle;
The Waves, as though the halcyon o'er its young
  Were always brooding, smile:

XVIII.

And every one that listens, presently
  Forgetteth home, and wife, and children dear,
All noble enterprise and purpose high,
  And turns his pinnace here—

XIX.

He turns his pinnace, warning taking none
From the plain doom of all that went before,
Whose bones lie bleaching in the wind and sun,
And whiten all the shore.*

XX.

He can not heed—so sweet unto him seems
To reap the harvest of the promised joy;
The wave-worn man of such secure rest dreams,
So guiltless of annoy.

XXI.

—The heroes and the kings, the wise, the strong,
That won the fleece with cunning and with might,
Their souls were taken in the net of song,
Snared in that false delight:

XXII.

Till ever loathlier seemed all toil to be,
And that small space they yet must travel o'er,
Stretched, an immeasurable breadth of sea,
Their fainting hearts before.

* Lord Bacon gives finely the inner meaning of this—namely: "Exempla calamitatum, licet clara et conspicua, contra voluptatum corruptelas non multum proficere."

XXIII.

“Let us turn hitherward our bark,” they cried,
“And, ’mid the blisses of this happy isle,
Past toil forgetting and to come, abide
In joyfulness awhile:

XXIV.

“And then, refreshed, our tasks resume again,
If other tasks we yet are bound unto,
Combing the hoary tresses of the main
With sharp, swift keel anew.”

XXV.

O heroes, that had once a nobler aim,
O heroes, sprung from many a godlike line,
What will ye do, unmindful of your fame,
And of your race divine?

XXVI.

But they, by these prevailing voices now
Lured, evermore draw nearer to the land;
Nor saw the wrecks of many a goodly prow,
That strewed that fatal strand:

XXVII.

Or seeing, feared not; warning taking none
From the plain doom of all who went before,
Whose bones lay bleaching in the wind and sun,
And whitened all the shore!

XXVIII.

And some impel through foaming billows now
  The hissing keel, and some tumultuous stand
Upon the deck, or crowd about the prow,
  Waiting to leap to land.

XXIX.

And them this fatal lodestar of delight
  Had drawn to ruin wholly, but for one
Of their own selves, who struck his lyre with might,
  Calliope's great son.

XXX.

He singing (for mere words were now in vain,
  That melody so led all souls at will),
Singing he played, and matched that earth-born strain
  With music sweeter still.

XXXI.

Of holier joy he sang, more true delight,
  In other, happier isles for them reserved,
Who, faithful here, from constancy, and right,
  And truth, have never swerved:

XXXII.

How evermore the tempered ocean-gales
  Breathe round those hidden islands of the blest,
Steeped in the glory spread, when daylight fails,
  Far in the sacred West:

XXXIII.

How unto them, beyond our mortal night,
  Shines evermore in strength the golden day;
And meadows with purpureal roses bright
  Bloom round their feet alway:

XXXIV.

And plants of gold—some burn beneath the sea,
  And some, for garlands apt, the land doth bear;
And lacks not many an incense-breathing tree,
  Enriching all that air.

XXXV.

Nor need is more, with sullen strength of hand
  To vex the stubborn earth, or plough the main;
They dwell apart, a calm, heroic band,
  Not tasting toil or pain.

XXXVI.

Nor sang he only of unfading bowers,
  Where they a tearless, painless age fulfil,
In fields Elysian spending blissful hours,
  Remote from every ill:

XXXVII.

But of pure gladness found in temperance high,
  In duty owned, and reverenced with awe,
Of man's true freedom, that may only lie
  In servitude to law:

XXXVIII.

And how 'twas given through virtue to aspire
  To golden seats in ever-calm abodes;
Of mortal men, admitted to the quire
  Of high, immortal gods.

XXXIX.

He sang—a mighty melody divine,
  That woke deep echoes in the heart of each—
Reminded whence they drew their royal line,
  And to what heights might reach.

XL.

And all the while they listened, them the speed
  Bore forward still of favoring wind and tide,
That, when their ears were vacant to give heed
  To any sound beside—

XLI.

The feeble echoes of that other lay,
  Which held awhile their senses thralled and bound,
Were in the distance fading quite away,
  A dull, unheeded sound.

QUATRAINS.

THE PHŒNIX.

WHEN Adam ate of that forbidden food,
  Sole bird that shared not in his sin was I;
And so my life is evermore renewed,
  And I among the dying never die.

THE PELICAN.

I am the bird that from my bleeding breast
  Draw the dear stream that nourishes my brood,
And feebly unto men his love attest,
  True pelican, that feeds them with his blood.

THE HALCYON.

For twice seven days, in winter's middle rage,
  The winds are hushed, the billows are at rest;
Heaven all for me their fury doth assuage,
  While I am brooding o'er my fluctuant nest.

THE COCK.

What time an ass with horrid bray you hear,
  Believe he sees a wicked sprite at hand;
But when I make my carol loud and clear,
  Know that an angel doth before me stand.

THE PEACOCK.

I, glorying in my tail's extended pride,
See my foul legs, and then I shriek outright:
So shrieks a human soul, that has descried
Its baseness 'mid vainglorious self-delight.

THE EAGLE.

I no degenerate progeny will raise,
But try my callow offspring, which will look
In the sun's eye with peremptory gaze,
Nor other nurslings in my nest will brook.

THE ERMINE.

To miry places me the hunters drive,
Where I my robes of purest white must stain;
Then yield I, nor for life will longer strive,
For spotless death ere spotted life is gain.

THE BEES.

We light on fruits and flowers, and purest things;
For if on carcases or aught unclean,
When homeward we returned, with mortal stings
Would slay us the keen watchers round our queen.

THE DIAMOND.

I only polished am in mine own dust—
Naught else against my hardness will prevail:
And thou, O man, in thine own sufferings must
Be polished: every meaner art will fail.

THE COCK.

I, clapping on my sides my wings with might,
First to myself the busy morn proclaim:
Who others doth to tasks and toil incite,
Should first himself have roused unto the same.

THE NIGHTINGALE.

Leaning my bosom on a pointed thorn,
I bleed, and bleeding sing my sweetest strain:
For sweetest songs of saddest hearts are born,
And who may here dissever love and pain?

THE SNAKE.

Myself I force some narrowest passage through,
Leaving my old and wrinkled skin behind,
And issuing forth in splendor of my new:
Hard entrance into life all creatures find.

THE TIGER.

Hearing sweet music, as in fell despite,
Himself the tiger doth in pieces tear:
The melody of other men's delight
There are, alas! who can as little bear.

FALLING STARS.

Angels are we, that, once from heaven exiled,
Would climb its crystal battlements again;
But have their keen-eyed watchers not beguiled,
Hurled by their glittering lances back amain.

THE OIL OF MERCY.

THE traditions of a relation between the tree of life which was set in Paradise, and the cross on which hung the Savior of the world, are almost infinite; or, rather, the one deep idea of their identity has clothed itself in innumerable forms. They constitute, indeed, one of the richest portions of what may perhaps without offence be termed the mythology of the Christian church. That which I have followed here is given in the "*Evangelium Nicodemi*," c. 19. (See Thilo's "*Codex Apocryphus*," v. i., p. 684.) In the "Recognitions" of Clement, l. 1, c. 45, an Ebionite book, and therefore only acknowledging the humanity of Christ, he is, consistently with this view, said, not himself to anoint, but to have been anointed with the oil from the tree of life. The connection between the tree of life and the cross of Christ has been twice wrought up into sublime dramatic poems by Calderon: once in his Auto, "*El Arbol del mejor Fruto*;" and again in that which is indeed only the same poem in a later and more perfect form, "*La Sibila del Oriente*." We have the same tradition of Seth going to the gates of Paradise in the fine old Cornish mystery, "The Creation of the World," which was published some years ago with an English translation; and allusions to it are frequent in all the popular literature of the middle ages: see, for instance, Goethe's recension of the "*Reineke Fuchs*," near the beginning of the tenth book; and a curious passage on the subject in Mandeville's "Travels." Rückert, in the poem which follows this, has given the tradition in somewhat a different shape. — I may just observe that this poem is an attempt — I will confess no very encouraging one — to write English verse in the Spanish assonant rhyme, of which the principle is, that words are considered to rhyme which have the same vowel-sounds, though the consonants are different; thus, *angel* and *raiment* having the same vowel-sounds, *a—e*, are perfect assonant rhymes. As in the Persian Ghazel, there is but one rhyme running through the whole poem, in which all the alternate lines, beginning with the second, terminate; and of course the rhythmical effect of the metre is to be judged, not by any half-dozen lines apart, but by the total impression which the whole poem continuously read leaves on the ear.

MANY beauteous spots the earth
Keepeth yet—but brighter, fairer
Did that long-lost Eden show
Than the loveliest that remaineth:
So what marvel, when our sire
Was from thence expelled, he waited
Lingering with a fond regret
Round those blessèd, happy places
Once his home, while innocence
Was his bright sufficient raiment?
Long he lingered there, and saw
Up from dark, abysmal spaces,
Four strong rivers rushing ever:
Saw the mighty wall exalted
High as heaven, and on its heights
Glimpses of the fiery angel!
Long he lingered near, with hope
Which had never quite abated,
That one day the righteous sentence,
Dooming him to stern disgraces,
Should be disannulled, and he
In his first bliss reinstated.
But when mortal pangs surprised him,
By an unseen foe assailèd,
Seth he called, his dearest son—

Called him to his side, and faintly
Him addressed: "My son, thou knowest
Of what sufferings partaker,
Of what weariness and toil,
Of what sickness, pain, and danger,
I have been, since that sad hour
That from Eden's precincts drave me.
But thou dost not know that God,
When to exile forth I farèd,
Houseless wanderer through the world,
Thus with gracious speech bespake me:
—'Though thou mayst not here continue,
In these blessèd, happy places,
As before from pain exempt,
Suffering, toil, and mortal ailment,
Think not thou shalt therefore be
Of my loving care forsaken:
Rather shall that tree of life,
In the middle garden planted,
Once a precious balm distil,
Which to thee applied, thine ailments
Shall be all removed, and thou
Made of endless life partaker.'—
With these words He cheered me then,
Words that have remained engraven
On my bosom's tablets since.
Go, then, dear my son, oh hasten
Unto Eden's guarded gate—

Tell thine errand to the angel;
And that fiery sentinel
To the tree will guide thee safely,
Where it stands, aloft, alone,
In the garden's middle spaces:
Thence bring back that oil of mercy,
Ere my lamp of life be wasted."

When his father's feeble words
Seth had heard, at once he hastened,
Hoping to bring back that oil,
Ere the light had wholly faded
From his father's eyes, the lamp
Of his life had wholly wasted.
O'er the plain besprent with flowers,
With ten thousand colors painted
In that spring-time of the year,
By Thelassar on he hastened,
Made no pause, till Eden's wall
Rose, an ever-verdant barrier,
High as heaven's great roof, that shines
With its bright carbuncles paven.
There the son of Adam paused,
For above him hung the angel
In the middle air suspense,
With his swift sword glancing naked.
Down upon his face he fell,
By the sun-bright vision dazèd.

"Child of man" — these words he heard —
"Rise, and say what thing thou cravest."

All his father's need he told,
And how now his father waited,
In his mighty agony
For that medicine yearning greatly.
"But thou seekest" — (this reply
Then he heard) — "thou seekest vainly
For that oil of mercy yet,
Nor will tears nor prayers avail thee.
Go then quickly back, and bring
These my words to him, thy parent,
Parent of the race of men.
He and they in faith and patience
Must abide; long years must be
Ere the precious fruit be gathered,
Ere the oil of mercy flow
From the blessèd tree and sacred,
In the Paradise of God:
Nor till then will be obtainèd
The strong medicine of life,
Healing every mortal ailment;
Nor thy sire till then be made
Of immortal life a sharer.
Fear not that his heart will sink
When these tidings back thou bearest;
Rather thou shalt straightway see

All his fears and pangs abated,
And by faith allayed to meekness
Every wish and thought impatient.
Hasten back, then—thy return,
Strongly yearning, he awaiteth:
Hasten back, then."—On the word,
To his father back he hastened;
Found him waiting his return
In his agony, his latest:
Told him of what grace to come,
Of what sure hope he was bearer;
And beheld him on that word,
Every fear and pang assuagèd,
And by faith allayed to meekness
Every wish and thought impatient,
Like a child resign himself
Unto sweet sleep, calm and painless.

THE TREE OF LIFE.

FROM THE GERMAN OF RUCKERT.

I.

WHEN Adam's latest breath was nearly gone,
To Paradise the patriarch sent his son—

II.

A branch to fetch him from the tree of life,
Hoping to taste of it ere life was done.

III.

Seth brought the branch, but, ere he had arrived,
His father's spirit was already flown.

IV.

Then planted they the twig on Adam's grave,
And it was tended still from son to son.

V.

It grew while Joseph in the dungeon lay,
It grew while Israel did in Egypt groan.

VI.

Sweet odors gave the blossoms of the tree,
When David harping sat upon his throne.

VII.

Dry was the tree, when from the ways of God
Went erring in his wisdom Solomon.

VIII.

Yet the world hoped it would revive anew,
When David's stock should give another Son.

IX.

Faith saw in spirit this, the while she sat
Mourning beside the floods of Babylon.

X.

And when the eternal lightning flashed from heaven,
The tree asunder burst with jubilant tone.

XI.

To the dry trunk this grace from God was given,
The Wood of Passion should from thence be won.

XII.

The blind world fashioned out of it the cross,
And its Salvation nailed with scorn thereon.

XIII.

Then bore the tree of life ensanguined fruit,
Which, whoso tasteth, life shall be his loan.

XIV.

Oh look, oh look, how grows the tree of life—
By storms established more, not overthrown!

XV.

May the *whole* world beneath its shadow rest!
Half has its shelter there already won.

THE TREE OF LIFE.

FROM AN OLD LATIN POEM.

I.

THERE is a spot, of men believed to be
Earth's centre, and the place of Adam's grave,
And here a slip that from a barren tree
Was cut, fruit sweet and salutary gave—
Yet not unto the tillers of the land;
That blessèd fruit was culled by other hand.

II.

The shape and fashion of the tree attend:
From undivided stem at first it sprung;
Thence in two arms its branches did outsend,
Like sail-yards whence the flowing sheet is hung,
Or as a yoke that in the furrow stands,
When the tired steers are loosened from their bands.

III.

Three days the slip from which this tree should spring
Appeared as dead—then suddenly it bore
(While earth and heaven stood awed and wondering)
Harvest of vital fruit;—the fortieth more
Beheld it touch heaven's summit with its height,
And shroud its sacred head in clouds of light.

IV.

Yet the same while it did put forth below
Branches twice six, these too with fruit endued,
Which, stretching to all quarters, might bestow
Upon all nations medicine and food,
Which mortal men might eat, and eating be
Sharers henceforth of immortality.

V.

But when another fifty days were gone,
A breath divine, a mighty storm of heaven,
On all the branches swiftly lighted down,
To which a rich, nectareous taste was given,
And all the heavy leaves that on them grew
Distilled henceforth a sweet and heavenly dew.

VI.

Beneath that tree's great shadow on the plain
A fountain bubbled up, whose lymph serene
Nothing of earthly mixture might distain:
Fountain so pure not anywhere was seen
In all the world, nor on whose marge the earth
Put flowers of such unfading beauty forth.

VII.

And thither did all people, young and old,
Matrons and virgins, rich and poor, a crowd
Stream ever, who, whenas they did behold
Those branches with their golden burden bowed,
Stretched forth their hands, and eager glances threw
Towàrd the fruit distilling that sweet dew.

VIII.

But touch they might not these, much less allay
Their hunger, howsoe'er they might desire,
Till the foul tokens of their former way
They had washed off, the dust and sordid mire,
And cleansed their bodies in that holy wave,
Able from every spot and stain to save.

IX.

But when within their mouths they had received
Of that immortal fruit the gust divine,
Straight of all sickness were their souls relieved,
The weak grew strong; and tasks they *did* decline
As overgreat for them, they shunned no more,
And things they deemed they could not bear, they bore.

X.

But wo, alas! some daring to draw near
That sacred stream, did presently retire,
Drew wholly back again, and did not fear
To stain themselves in all their former mire—
That fruit rejecting from their mouths again,
Not any more their medicine, but their bane.

XI.

Oh, blessèd they, who not withdrawing so,
First in that fountain make them pure and fair,
And who from thence unto the branches go,
With power upon the fruitage hanging there:
Thence by the branches of the lofty tree
Ascend to heaven—The Tree of Life oh, see!

THE HOLY EUCHARIST.

FROM CALDERON.

HONEY in the lion's mouth,
Emblem mystical, divine,
How the sweet and strong combine!
Cloven rock for Israel's drouth;
Treasure-house of golden grain,
By our Joseph laid in store,
In his brethren's famine sore
Freely to dispense again;
Dew on Gideon's snowy fleece;
Well from bitter changed to sweet;
Show-bread laid in order meet—
Bread whose cost doth ne'er increase,
Though no rain in April fall;
Horeb's manna, freely given,
Showered in white dew from heaven,
Marvellous, angelical;
Weightiest bunch of Canaan's vine;
Cake to strengthen and sustain
Through long days of desert pain;
Salem's monarch's bread and wine;—
Thou the antidote shalt be
Of my sickness and my sin,
Consolation, medicine,
Life and sacrament, to me.

THE PRODIGAL.

I.

WHY feedest thou on husks so coarse and rude?
I could not be content with angels' food.

II.

How camest thou companion to the swine?
I loathed the courts of heaven, the choir divine.

III.

Who bade thee crouch in hovel dark and drear?
I left a palace wide to sojourn here.

IV.

Harsh tyrant's slave who made thee, once so free?
A father's rule too heavy seemed to me.

V.

What sordid rags hang round thee on the breeze?
I laid immortal robes aside for these.

VI.

An exile through the world who bade thee roam?
None, but I wearied of a happy home.

VII.

Why must thou dweller in a desert be?
A garden seemed not fair enough to me.

VIII.

Why sue a beggar at the mean world's door?
To live on God's large bounty seemed so poor.

IX.

What has thy forehead so to earthward brought?
To lift it higher than the stars I thought.

LINES

WRITTEN ON THE FIRST TIDINGS OF THE CABUL MASSACRES, JANUARY, 1842.

I.

WE sat our peaceful hearths beside;
Within our temples hushed and wide
We worshipped without fear:
With solemn rite, with festal blaze,
We welcomed in the earliest days
Of this new-coming year.

II.

O ye that died, brave hearts and true,
How in those days it fared with you
We did not then surmise;
That bloody rout, which still doth seem
The fancy of a horrid dream,
Was hidden from our eyes:

III.

But haunts us now by day and night
The vision of that ghastly flight,
In shapes of haggard fear:

While still from many a mourning home
The wails of lamentation come,
  And fill our saddened ear.

IV.

O England, bleeding at thy heart
For thy lost sons, a solemn part
  Doth Heaven to thee assign!
High wisdom hast thou need to ask,
For vengeance is a fearful task,
  And yet that task is thine.

V.

Oh, then, fulfil it, not in pride,
Nor aught to passionate hate allied;
  But know thyself to be
The justicer of righteous Heaven;
That unto thee a work is given,
  A burden laid on thee.

VI.

So thine own heart from guilty stains
First cleanse, and then, for what remains,
  That do with all thy might;
That with no faltering hand fulfil,
With no misgiving heart or will,
  As dubious of the right;

VII.

That do, not answering wrong for wrong,
But witnessing that truth is strong,
  And, outraged, bringeth wo.
'Tis this by lessons sad and stern,
To men who no way else would learn,
  Which thou art set to show.

MOOLTAN.

"A COMPANY of Moolraj's Muzubees, or outcasts turned Sikhs, led on the mob. It was an appalling sight; and Sirdar Khan Sing begged of Mr. Agnew to be allowed to wave a sheet, and sue for mercy. Weak in body from loss of blood, Agnew's heart failed him not. He replied: 'The time for mercy is gone; let none be asked for. They can kill us two if they like, but we are not the last of the English: thousands of Englishmen will come down here when we are gone, and annihilate Moolraj, and his soldiers, and his fort!' The crowd now rushed in with horrible shouts; made Khan Sing prisoner, and, pushing aside the servants with the butts of their muskets, surrounded the two wounded officers. Lieutenant Anderson, from the first, had been too much wounded even to move; and now Mr. Agnew was sitting by his bedside, holding his hand, and talking in English. Doubtless, they were bidding each other farewell for all time. . . . . Anderson was hacked to death with swords, and afterward the two bodies were dragged outside, and slashed and insulted by the crowd; then left all night under the sky."—*Major Edwardes' "Year on the Punjaub Frontier,"* vol. ii., p. 58.

"The besieging army did not march away to other fields without performing its last melancholy duty to the memory of Agnew and Anderson. The bodies of those officers were carefully—I may say affectionately—removed from the careless grave where they lay side by side; and, wrapped in Cashmere shawls (with a vain but natural desire to obliterate all traces of neglect), were borne by the soldiers of the 1st Bombay Fusileers (Anderson's own regiment) to an honored resting-place on the summit of Moolraj's citadel. By what way borne? Through the gate where they had been first assaulted? Oh, no! through the broad and sloping breach which had been made by the British guns in the walls of the rebellious fortress of Mooltan."—*Ib.*, p. 588.

I.

BEAR them gently, bear them duly up the broad and
sloping breach
Of this torn and shattered city, till their resting-place
they reach.

II.

In the costly cashmeres folded, on the stronghold's top-
most crown,
In the place of foremost honor, lay these noble relics
down.

III.

Here repose, for this is meetest, ye who here breathed
out your life—
Ah! in no triumphant battle, but beneath the assassin's
knife.

IV.

Hither bearing England's message, bringing England's
just command,
Under England's ægis, came ye to the chieftain of the
land:

V.

In these streets beset and wounded, hardly borne with
life away—
Faint, and bleeding, and forsaken, in your helplessness
ye lay.

VI.

But the wolves that once have tasted blood, will ravin still for more;
From the infuriate city rises high the wild and savage roar.

VII.

Near and nearer grows the tumult of the gathering, murderous crew;
Tremble round those helpless couches an unarmed but faithful few:

VIII.

"Profitless is all resistance: let us, then, this white flag wave;
Ere it be too late, disdain not mercy at their hands to crave."

IX.

But to no unworthy pleading would descend that noble twain:—
"Nay, for mercy sue not; ask not what to ask from these were vain.

X.

"We are two, betrayed and lonely; human help or hope is none;
Yet, O friends, be sure that England owns beside us many a son.

XI.

"They may slay us: in our places multitudes will here
be found,
Strong to hurl this guilty city with its murderers to the
ground!

XII.

"Yea, who stone by stone would tear it from its deep
foundations strong,
Rather than to leave unpunished them that wrought this
bloody wrong."

XIII.

Other words they changed between them, which none else
could understand—
Accents of our native English, brothers grasping hand in
hand.

XIV.

So they died, the gallant-hearted! so from earth their
spirits past,
Uttering words of lofty comfort each to each unto the
last:

XV.

And we heed, but little heeded their true spirits far
away,
All of wrong and coward outrage, heaped on the unfeeling
clay!

XVI.

—Lo! a few short moons have vanished, and the promised ones appear;
England's pledged and promised thousands, England's multitudes are here.

XVII.

Flame around the blood-stained ramparts swiftest messengers of death,
Girdling with a fiery girdle—blasting with a fiery breath!—

XVIII.

Ceasing not, till, choked with corpses, low is laid the murderers' hold,
And in his last lair the tiger toils of righteous wrath enfold.

XIX.

Well, oh well!—ye have not failed them who on England's truth relied—
Who on England's name and honor did in that dread hour confide:

XX.

Now one last dear duty render to the faithful and the brave,
What they left of earth behind them rescuing for a worthier grave.

XXI.

Oh, then, bear them, hosts of England, up the broad and sloping breach
Of this torn and shattered city, till their resting-place they reach.

XXII.

In the costly cashmeres folded, on the rampart's topmost crown,
In the place of foremost honor, lay these noble relics down.

SONNET.

ULYSSES, sailing by the Sirens' isle,
Sealed first his comrades' ears, then bade them fast
Bind him with many a fetter to the mast,
Lest those sweet voices should their souls beguile,
And to their ruin flatter them, the while
Their homeward bark was sailing swiftly past;
And thus the peril they behind them cast,
Though chased by those weird voices many a mile.
But yet a nobler cunning Orpheus used:
No fetter he put on, nor stopped his ear;
But ever, as he passed, sang high and clear
The blisses of the gods, their holy joys,
And with diviner melody confused
And marred earth's sweetest music to a noise.

THE ETRURIAN KING.

SEE Mrs. Hamilton Gray's "Visit to the Sepulchres of Etruria."

I.

ONE only eye beheld him in his pride,
The old Etrurian monarch, as he died—

II.

And as they laid him on his bier of stone,
Shield, spear, and arrows, laying at his side—

III.

In golden armor, with his crown of gold,
One only eye the kingly warrior spied:

IV.

Nor that eye long—for in the common air
The wondrous pageant might not now abide—

V.

Which had in sealèd sepulchre the wrongs
Of time for thirty centuries defied.

VI.

That eye beheld it melt and disappear,
As down an hour-glass the last sand-drops glide.

VII.

A few short moments—and a shrunken heap
Of common dust survived, of all that pride.

VIII.

And so that gorgeous vision has remained
For evermore to other eye denied:

IX.

And he who saw must oftentimes believe
That him his waking senses had belied:

X.

Since what if all the pageants of the earth
Melt soon away, and may not long abide—

XI.

Yet when did ever doom *so* swift before
Even to the glories of the world betide?

THE PRIZE OF SONG.

I.

CHALLENGED by the haughty daughters
  Of the old Emathian king,
Strove the Muses at the waters
  Of that Heliconian spring—
Proved beside those hallowed fountains
  Unto whom the prize of song,
Unto whom those streams and mountains,
  Did of truest right belong.

II.

First those others in vexed numbers
  Mourned the rebel giant brood,
Whom the earth's huge mass encumbers,
  Or who writhe, the vulture's food;
Mourned for earth-born power, which faileth
  Heaven to win by might and main;
Then, thrust back, for ever waileth,
  Gnawing its own heart in pain.

III.

Nature shuddered while she hearkened,
  Through her veins swift horror ran:
Sun and stars, perturbed and darkened,
  To forsake their orbs began.
Back the rivers fled; the ocean
  Howled upon a thousand shores,
As it would with wild commotion
  Burst its everlasting doors.

IV.

Hushed was not that stormy riot,
  Till were heard the sacred Nine,
Singing of the blissful quiet
  In the happy seats divine;
Singing of those thrones immortal,
  Whither struggling men attain,
Passing humbly through the portal
  Of obedience, toil, and pain.

V.

At that melody symphonious
  Joy to Nature's heart was sent,
And the spheres, again harmonious,
  Made sweet thunder as they went:
Lightly moved, with pleasure dancing,
  Little hills and mountains high—
Helicon his head advancing,
  Till it almost touched the sky.

VI.

—Thou whom once those Sisters holy
  On thy lonely path hath met,
And, thy front thou stooping lowly,
  There their sacred laurel set—
Oh, be thine, their mandate owning,
  Aye with them to win the prize,
Reconciling and atoning
  With thy magic harmonies:

VII.

An Arion thou, whose singing
  Rouses not a furious sea—
Rather the sea-monsters bringing
  Servants to its melody;
An Amphion, not with passion
  To set wild the builders' mind,
But the mystic walls to fashion,
  And the stones in one to bind.

I.

O LIFE, O Death, O World, O Time,
  O Grave, where all things flow,
'Tis yours to make our lot sublime,
  With your great weight of wo!

II.

Though sharpest anguish hearts may wring,
  Though bosoms torn may be,
Yet suffering is a holy thing;
  Without it what were we?

JANUARY 16, 1841.

I.

NO mother's eye beside thee wakes to-night,
No taper burns beside thy lonely bed;
Darkling thou liest, hidden out of sight,
And none are near thee but the silent dead.

II.

How cheerly glows this hearth, yet glows in vain,
For we uncheered beside it sit alone,
And listen to the wild and beating rain
In angry gusts against our casement blown:

III.

And though we nothing speak, yet well I know
That both our hearts are there, where thou dost keep
Within thy narrow chamber far below,
For the first time unwatched, thy lonely sleep:

IV.

Oh no, not thou!—and we our faith deny,
This thought allowing: thou, removed from harms,
In Abraham's bosom dost securely lie;
Oh! not in Abraham's, in a Savior's arms—

V.

In that dear Lord's, who, in thy worst distress,
Thy bitterest anguish, gave thee, dearest child,
Still to abide in perfect gentleness,
And like an angel to be meek and mild.

VI.

Sweet corn of wheat, committed to the ground
To die, and live, and bear more precious ear,
While in the heart of earth thy Savior found
His place of rest, for thee we will not fear.

VII.

Sleep softly, till that blessèd rain and dew,
Down lighting upon earth, such change shall bring,
That all its fields of death shall laugh anew—
Yea, with a living harvest laugh and sing.

I.

WHAT was thy life? a pearl cast up awhile
Upon the bank and shoal of Time;—again,
Even as did the gazers' eyes beguile,
To be drawn backward by the hungry main.

II.

What was thy life? a fountain of sweet wave,
Which to the salt sea's margin all too near
Rose sparkling, and a few steps scarcely gave,
Ere *that* distained its waters fresh and clear.

III.

What was thy life? a flowering almond-tree,
Which all too soon its blossoms did unfold;
And so must see their lustre presently
Dimmed, and their beauty nipped by envious cold.

IV.

What was thy life? a bright and beauteous flame,
  Wherein, a season, light and joy we found;
But a swift sound of rushing tempest came,
  It past—and sparkless ashes strewed the ground!

V.

What was thy life? a bird in infant's hand
  Held with too slight a grasp, and which, before
He knows or fears, its pinions doth expand,
  And with a sudden impulse heavenward soar.

I.

I CAN NOT tell what coming years
May have, reserved, of grief for me;
I can not tell what they may be—
How rung with anguish, dimmed with tears:

II.

But scarcely can a sadder morn
Than this upon mine eyelids break,
When from a flattering dream I wake
On a reality forlorn.

III.

For never from thine ivory gate,
O Sleep, a falser dream was sent
Than unto me brief gladness lent,
To leave me sorrow's trustier mate.

IV.

We wandered freely as of yore,
 And in my hand I felt the grasp
 Of that small hand, whose tender clasp
I shall not feel, oh! any more:

V.

We wandered through the peopled towns,
 And where we came I heard men praise
 His gracious looks, his winning ways—
We wandered o'er the lonely downs:

VI.

And ever held familiar talk
 As we passed onward, I and he—
 Who was companion true to me
At home, and in long woodland walk:

VII.

Gone was the agony, the fear,
 And all the dreadful gulf between
 What we are now and what have been,
The vault, the coffin, and the bier.

VIII.

I start—and lo! my dream is not:
 But though 'tis round me thickest gloom,
 Yet in the corner of the room
I know there stands a vacant cot.

IX.

I close mine eyes—I strive again
To feed upon that poor delight:
The broken links to reunite
Once more of slumber's golden chain.

X.

Lost effort!—Sleep, oh! twice untrue,
What need to bring that fond deceit?
And then, when I allow the cheat,
To flee, while vainly I pursue?

TO ——.

I.

WE did not quite believe this world would give
To us what ne'er it had to any given—
That round our bark eternal calms should live,
That ours should ever be a stormless heaven:

II.

Yet we, long season, were like men that dwell
In safe abodes beside some perilous shore,
Who, when they hear the northern whirlwinds swell—
Who, when they hear the furious breakers roar—

III.

Think, it may be, but with too slight a thought,
On them that in the great deep laboring are,
Where winds are high, and waves are madly wrought—
And lend them, it may be, a passing prayer.

IV.

Thus we, belovèd, in our safe recess
  Did evermore abroad the voices hear,
In the great world, of sorrow and distress,
  With pity heard, yet us they came not near:

V.

Or if at times they might approach us nigh,
  And if at times we mourned, yet still remained
Our inner world untouched—the sanctuary
  Of our blest home by sorrow unprofaned—

VI.

When lo! that cup which we had seen go round
  To one and to another, cup of pain,
We of a sudden at our own lips found,
  And it was given us deep of that to drain:

VII.

And what had seemed at first a little cloud
  On our clear sky, no broader than the hand,
Did all its lights and constellations shroud,
  And gloomy wings from end to end expand.

VIII.

O unforgotten day! the earliest morn
  Of the new year, when friends are wont to meet,
And while upon all faces joy is worn,
  Each doth the other with kind wishes greet—

IX.

O day, whose anguish never shall wax old,
  When we no longer might our fears deny,
When our hearts' secret thoughts we dared unfold
  One to the other, that our child would die.

X.

Oh! freshly may in us the memory live
  Of the mere lie, which then the world did seem,
And all the world could promise or could give—
  A breaking bubble! a departing dream!

XI.

So while this lore doth in our hearts remain,
  We on the world shall lean not, that false reed,
Not strong enough our burden to sustain,
  Yet sharp enough to pierce us till we bleed.

XII.

But now a pearl is from our chaplet dropped,
  But now a flower is from our garland riven,
One singing fountain of our joy is stopped,
  One brightest star extinguished in our heaven—

XIII.

One only—yet, oh! who may guess the change
  That by that one has been among us wrought?
How all familiar things are waxen strange
  Or sad—what silence to our house is brought?

XIV.

Or if the merry voices still arise,
  Now that the captain of the games is gone,
We check them not, but still into our eyes
  The tears have started at that alien tone:

XV.

And we, perchance too confident of old,
  As though our blessings all were ours in fee,
Those that remain now tremulously hold,
  From anxious perturbations never free—

XVI.

As though the spell were broken, and the charm
  Reversed, which shielded had our house so long,
And we without defence to every harm
  Lay open, and exposed to every wrong.

XVII.

Oh! thought which should not be, oh! faith too weak,
  To tremble at the slightest ache or pain,
At the least languor of the changeful cheek,
  With terrors hardly to be stilled again.

XVIII.

Yet thus we walk within our house, in grief
  For what has been, in fear for what may be,
And still the advancing days bring no relief,
  But make us all our loss more plainly see.

XIX.

And when this pallid winding-sheet of snow,
Which all this dreary time the earth has wound,
Dissolves and disappears, as warm winds blow,
And the hard soil, relenting, is unbound—

XX.

And when that happy season shall arrive,
To mourning hearts the saddest in its mirth,
When all things in this living world revive,
Save the dear clod low-lying in the earth—

XXI.

We shall bethink us then with what delight
He used to hail, himself discovering first,
The purple or the yellow crocus bright,
Or where the snowdrop from its sheath had burst.

XXII.

Oh! then shall I remember many a walk
In shadowy woods, close hidden from the flames
Of the fierce sun, and interspersed with talk
Of ancient England's high, heroic names:

XXIII.

Or, holier still, of them who lived and died,
That Christ's dear lore to us they might hand down
Untarnished, or his faith to spread more wide,
Winning a martyr's palms and martyr's crown:

XXIV.

Or how those tales he earnestly would crave
  Of old romance, our childhood's golden dower,
Which in large measure willingly we gave,
  Feeding the pure, imaginative power.

XXV.

O days that never, never shall return!
  The future may be rich in genial good,
We are not poor in hope, we do not mourn
  The wreck of all our bliss around us strewed:

XXVI.

Oh, no—fair flowrets blossom in our bowers,
  Rich pearls upon our chaplet still are given,
And singing fountains of delight are ours,
  And stars of brightness in our earthly heaven.

XXVII.

Yet never can that golden time come back,
  When we could look around us with an eye
Entirely satisfied, which did not lack
  One of the happy number standing by:

XXVIII.

When yet no edge as of encroaching dark,
  Gave token that our moon began to wane,
When the most curious eye had failed to mark
  Upon its clear, bright surface speck or stain.

XXIX.

—Lo! as that bird which all the wakeful night
  Leaning its bosom on a piersant thorn,
So bleeds, and bleeding sings, and makes delight
  For some that listen, though its heart be torn—

XXX.

Thus in this night of sorrow I do lean
  With wounded bosom, and so make my song,
Upon the thorn of memories sharp and keen,
  Well pleasèd while I do myself this wrong.

XXXI.

And yet, belovèd, why should we lament
  That vanished time with passionate regret—
Not rather marvelling at the rare consent
  Of blessings which so long above us met?

XXXII.

Oh! lot which could not aye endure—oh! lot
  Which could not be for sinful men designed;
For we, not suffering, should have quite forgot
  To feel or suffer with our suffering kind:

XXXIII.

Oh! lot it was to waken liveliest fears,
  A lot which never have God's servants known;—
Yea, who amid a world of grief and tears,
  In freedom from all pain would stand alone?

XXXIV.

And what though now we from this grief express
 But little save its bitter, yet be sure
In this its mere unmingled bitterness
 It shall not, can not evermore endure.

XXXV.

But comforts shall arise, like fountains sweet
 Fresh springing in a salt and dreary main,
Fountains of sweetest wave, which shipmen meet
 In the waste ocean, an unlooked-for gain.

XXXVI.

And as when some fair temple is o'erthrown
 By earthquake, or by hostile hand laid waste,
At first it lies, stone rudely rent from stone,
 A confused, ruinous heap, and all defaced:

XXXVII.

Yet visit that fallen ruin by-and-by,
 And what a hand of healing has been there!
How sweetly do the placid sunbeams lie
 On the green sward which all the place doth wear!

XXXVIII.

And what rich odors from the flowers are borne,
 From flowers and flowering weeds which even within
The rents and fissures of those walls forlorn
 Have made their home, yea thence their sustenance win!

XXXIX.

So time no less has gentle skill to heal
  When our fair hopes have fallen, our earth-built towers,
How busy wreck and ruin to conceal
  With a new overgrowth of leaves and flowers.

XL.

Nor time alone—a better hand is here,
  Where it has wounded, watching to upbind,
Which when it takes away in love severe,
  Doth some austerer blessing leave behind.

XLI.

Oh! higher gifts has brought this mournful time,
  Than all those years which did so smoothly run:
For what if they, life's flower and golden prime,
  Had something served to knit our hearts in one?—

XLII.

Yet doth that all seem little now, compared
  With our brief fellowship in tears and pain;
To share the things which we have newly shared,
  This makes a firmer bond, a holier chain:

XLIII.

To have together held that aching head,
  To have together heard that piteous moan,
To have together knelt beside that bed,
  When life was flitting, and when life had flown—

XLIV.

And to have one of ours, whose ashes sleep
  Where the great church its solemn shadow flings —
Oh! love has now its roots that stretch more deep,
  That strike and stretch beneath the grave of things.

XLV.

Oh! more than this, yet holier bonds there are,
  For we his spirit shall to ours feel nigh,
And know he lives, whenever we in prayer
  Hold with heaven's saintly throng communion high.

XLVI.

Then wherefore more? — or wherefore this to thee —
  A faithful suppliant at that inner shrine,
At which who kneel, to them 'tis given see
  How pain, and grief, and anguish, are divine?

"What pang is permanent with man? From the highest,
As from the meanest thing of every day,
He learns to wean himself: for the strong hours
Conquer him."

I.

WHO that a watcher doth remain
Beside a couch of mortal pain,
Deems he can ever smile again?

II.

Or who that weeps beside a bier
Counts he has any more to fear
From the world's flatteries, false and leer?

III.

And yet anon and he doth start
At the light toys in which his heart
Can now already claim its part.

IV.

O hearts of ours! so weak and poor,
That nothing there can long endure;
And so their hurts find shameful cure—

V.

While every sadder, wiser thought,
Each holier aim which sorrow brought,
Fades quite away and comes to naught.

VI.

O Thou, who dost our weakness know,
Watch for us, that the strong hours so
Not wean us from our wholesome wo.

VII.

Grant Thou that we may long retain
The wholesome memories of pain,
Nor wish to lose them soon again.

I.

THAT name! how often every day
We spake it and we heard!
It was to us, 'mid tasks or play,
A common household word.

II.

'Tis breathèd yet, that name—but oh,
How solemn now the sound!—
One of the sanctities which throw
Such awe our homes around.

THE LENT JEWELS.

A JEWISH TALE.

IN schools of wisdom all the day was spent:
His steps at eve the Rabbi homeward bent,
With homeward thoughts, which dwelt upon the wife
And two fair children who consoled his life.
She, meeting at the threshold, led him in,
And with these words preventing, did begin:—
"Ever rejoicing at your wished return,
Yet am I most so now: for since this morn
I have been much perplexed and sorely tried
Upon one point which you shall now decide.
Some years ago, a friend into my care
Some jewels gave—rich, precious gems they were;
But having given them in my charge, this friend
Did afterward nor come for them, nor send,
But left them in my keeping for so long,
That now it almost seems to me a wrong
That he should suddenly arrive to-day,
To take those jewels, which he left, away.
What think you? Shall I freely yield them back,
And with no murmuring?—so henceforth to lack

Those gems myself, which I had learned to see
Almost as mine for ever, mine in fee."

"What question can be here? Your own true heart
Must needs advise you of the only part:
That may be claimed again which was but lent,
And should be yielded with no discontent.
Nor surely can we find herein a wrong,
That it was left us to enjoy it long."

"Good is the word," she answered; "may we now
And evermore that it is good allow!"
And, rising, to an inner chamber led,
And there she showed him, stretched upon one bed,
Two children pale: and he the jewels knew,
Which God had lent him, and resumed anew.

ON THE DEATH OF AN INFANT.

'MID sterner losses let us own this gain—
An infant this will evermore remain:
Those other, should they reach life's longer date,
In them the coming will obliterate
The past; and we shall what they were forget,
Our eyes upon their later semblance set;
But this remaineth an eternal child.
Might sorrow for a little be beguiled,
Even with this thought a soothing fancy brings!
Her image has escaped the flux of things,
And that same infant beauty which she wore
Is fixed upon her now for evermore—
The everlasting garment fresh and new
Which in our eyes will ever her endue,
Which she will not put off, as the others must,
For garments soilèd more with this world's dust:
As though a bud should be a bud for ever,
A crystal rill ne'er swell to turbid river;
As though on aught most fleeting and most fair,
The roseate tints which clouds of evening wear,
We might lay hands on, and fix them ever there.

ALMA.

THOUGH till now ungraced in story, scant although
thy waters be,
Alma, roll those waters proudly, proudly roll them to
the sea!

Yesterday unnamed, unhonored, but to wandering Tartar
known,
Now thou art a voice for ever, to the world's four corners
blown.

In two nations' annals graven, thou art now a deathless
name,
And a star for ever shining in their firmament of fame.

Many a great and ancient river, crowned with city, tower,
and shrine,
Little streamlet, knows no magic, boasts no potency like
thine:

Can not shed the light thou sheddest around many a living
head—
Can not lend the light thou lendest to the memories of the
dead.

Yea, nor all unsoothed their sorrow, who can, proudly mourning, say—
When the first strong burst of anguish shall have wept itself away:—

"He has passed from us, the loved one; but he sleeps with them that died
By the Alma, at the winning of that terrible hillside!"

Yes, and in the days far onward, when we all are cold as those,
Who beneath thy vines and willows on their hero-beds repose—

Thou on England's banners blazoned with the famous fields of old,
Shalt, where other fields are winning, wave above the brave and bold:

And our sons unborn shall nerve them for some great deed to be done,
By that twentieth of September, when the Alma's heights were won.

O thou river! dear for ever to the gallant, to the free,
Alma, roll thy waters proudly, proudly roll them to the sea.

AFTER THE BATTLE.

WE crowned the hard-won heights at length,
Baptized in flame and fire;
We saw the foeman's sullen strength,
That grimly made retire—

Saw close at hand, then saw more far
Beneath the battle-smoke
The ridges of his shattered war,
That broke and ever broke.

But one, an English household's pride,
Dear many ways to me,
Who climbed that death-path by my side,
I sought, but could not see.

Last seen, what time our foremost rank
That iron tempest tore;
He touched, he scaled the rampart bank—
Seen then, and seen no more.

One friend to aid, I measured back
With him that pathway dread;
No fear to wander from our track—
Its waymarks English dead.

Light thickened: but our search was crowned,
As we too well divined;
And after briefest quest we found
What we most feared to find.

His bosom with one death-shot riven,
The warrior-boy lay low;
His face was turned unto the heaven,
His feet unto the foe.

As he had fallen upon the plain,
Inviolate he lay;
No ruffian spoiler's hand profane
Had touched that noble clay.

And precious things he still retained,
Which, by one distant hearth,
Loved tokens of the loved, had gained
A worth beyond all worth.

I treasured these for them who yet
Knew not their mighty wo;
I softly sealed his eyes, and set
One kiss upon his brow.

A decent grave we scooped him, where
Less thickly lay the dead,
And decently composed him there
Within that narrow bed.

O theme for manhood's bitter tears—
The beauty and the bloom
Of less than twenty summer years
Shut in that darksome tomb!

Of soldier-sire the soldier-son—
Life's honored eventide
One lives to close in England, one
In maiden battle died:

And they that should have been the mourned,
The mourners' parts obtain:
Such thoughts were ours, as we returned
To earth its earth again.

Brief words we read of faith and prayer
Beside that hasty grave;
Then turned away, and left him there,
The gentle and the brave:

I calling back with thankful heart,
With thoughts to peace allied,
Hours when we two had knelt apart
Upon the lone hillside—

And, comforted, I praised the grace
Which him had led to be
An early seeker of that Face
Which he should early see.

BALAKLAVA.

MANY a deed of faithful daring may obtain no record here,
Wrought where none could see or note it, save the one Almighty Seer.

Many a deed awhile remembered, out of memory needs must fall,
Covered, as the years roll onward, by oblivion's creeping pall:

But there are which never, never to oblivion can give room,
Till in flame earth's records perish, till the thunder-peal of doom.

And of these through all the ages married to immortal fame,
One is linked, and linked for ever, Balaklava, with thy name—

With thine armies three that wondering stood at gaze and held their breath,
With thy fatal lists of honor, and thy tournament of death.

O our brothers that are sleeping, weary with your great
day's strife,
On that bleak Crimean headland, noble prodigals of life—

Eyes which ne'er beheld you living, these have dearly
mourned you dead,
All your squandered wealth of valor, all the lavish blood
ye shed.

And in our eyes tears are springing, but we bid them
back again;
None shall say, to see us weeping, that we hold your
offering vain:

That for nothing, in our sentence, did that holocaust arise,
With a battle-field for altar, and with you for sacrifice.

Not for naught; to more than warriors armed as you for
mortal fray,
Unto each that in life's battle waits his Captain's word
ye say:—

"What by duty's voice is bidden, there where duty's star
may guide,
Thither follow, that accomplish, whatsoever else betide."

This ye taught; and this your lesson solemnly in blood
ye sealed:
Heroes, martyrs, are the harvest Balaklava's heights shall
yield.

’Η ΤΑΝ, ’Η ’ΕΠΙ ΤΑΝ.

"THIS, *or on this!*"—"Bring home with thee this shield,
Or be thou, dead, upon this shield brought home!"
So spake the Spartan mother to the son
Whom her own hands had armed. O strong of heart!
Yet know I of a fairer strength than this —
Strength linked with weakness, steeped in tears and fears,
And tenderness of trembling womanhood;
But true as hers to duty's perfect law.
And such is theirs who in our England now,
Wives, sisters, mothers, watch by day, by night,
In many a cottage, many a stately hall,
For those dread posts, too slow, too swift, that haste
O'er land and sea, the messengers of doom;
Theirs, who ten thousand times would rather hear
Of loved forms stretched upon the bloody sod,
All cold and stark, but with the debt they owed
To that dear land that bore them duly paid,
Than look to enfold them in fond arms again,
By aught in honor's or in peril's path
Unduly shunned, reserved for that embrace.

SUNDAY, NOVEMBER THE FIFTH, 1854.

CHEERLY with us that great November morn
  Rose, as I trace its features in my mind;
A day that, in the lap of winter born,
  Yet told of autumn scarcely left behind.

And we by many a hearth in all the land,
  Whom quiet sleep had lapped the calm night through,
Changed greetings, lip with lip, and hand to hand,
  Old greetings, but which love makes ever new.

Then, as the day brought with it sweet release
  From this world's care, with timely feet we trod
The customary paths of blessèd peace,
  We worshipped in the temples of our God:

And when the sun had travelled his brief arc,
  Drew round our hearths again in thankful ease;
With pleasant light we chased away the dark,
  We sat at eve with children round our knees.

So fared this day with us;—but how with you?
  What, gallant hosts of England, was your cheer,
Who numbered hearts as gentle and as true
  As any kneeling at our altars here?

From cheerless watches on the cold, dank ground
  Startled, ye felt a foe on every side;
With mist, and gloom, and deaths, encompassed round,
  With even to perish in the light denied.

And that same season of our genial ease,
  It was your very agony of strife;
While each of those our golden moments sees
  With you the ebbing of some noble life.

'Mid dark ravines, by precipices vast,
  Did there and here your dreadful conflict sway:
No sabbath day's light work to quell at last
  The fearful odds of that unequal fray.

O "hope" of England, only not "forlorn"
  Because ye never your own hope resigned,
But in worst case, beleagured, overborne,
  Did help in God and in your own selves find—

We greet you o'er the waves, as from this time
  Men, to the meanest and the least of whom,
In reverence of fortitude sublime,
  We would rise up, and yield respectful room:

We greet you o'er the waves, nor fear to say,
  Our sabbath setting side by side with yours,
Yours was the better and far nobler day,
  And days like it have made that ours endures.

THE END.

www.ingramcontent.com/pod-product-compliance
Lightning Source LLC
LaVergne TN
LVHW020211110826
845151LV00003B/677

* 9 7 8 1 4 2 5 5 3 3 6 5 6 *